The Way of a Yacht

'There are three things which are too wonderful
for me, yea, four which I know not:
     'The way of an eagle in the air; the way
of a serpent upon a rock; the way of a ship in the
midst of the sea; and the way of a man with a maid.'

PROVERBS 30:18,19
ascribed to Solomon *c.* 960 BC

'Yacht design as carried on at the present is
rather like making love to a woman. The approach is
completely empirical. At the end, the male, even
though he might be successful, usually has no idea
of just how and why he had succeeded.'

Professor E. J. RICHARDS
University of Southampton
Conference on Yacht Design
1962

The Way of a Yacht

An introduction to the comparative anatomy of offshore sailing craft

Alan Hollingsworth

W W Norton & Company Inc

New York, New York

TO THE OFFSHORE RACING CREWS OF THE

Royal Air Force

WHO HAVE REPEATEDLY PROVED THEIR WORTH
IN SMALL BOATS UNLIKE THOSE TRADITIONAL
ENCUMBRANCES — STEPLADDERS, WHEELBARROWS,
et al

First American edition 1974

ISBN 0-393-03181-0

Printed in Great Britain

Contents

List of Illustrations

Abbreviations

V_s	Ship velocity – speed and direction
V_{mg}	Velocity made good to windward
V_T	Velocity of true wind
V_A	Velocity of apparent wind
γ	True windcourse (angle)
β	Apparent windcourse (angle)
ε	Aerodynamic drag angle
δ	Hydrodynamic drag angle
λ	Leeway angle
R_A	Resultant force – air
R_W	Resultant force – water
LOA	Length overall
LWL	Load waterline length
B	Beam
B_{max}	Maximum beam
D	Depth of hull
S, SA	Sail area
AR	Aspect ratio
W	Weight, displacement
RORC	Royal Ocean Racing Club
CCA	Cruising Club of America
IOR	International Offshore Rule
ORC	Offshore Rating Council

Preface

Who contributes most to winning races – the crew or the yacht? There is, of course, no answer, for the two are inseparable. The actions of the one bring a response in the other that can be likened to that of a well-attuned horse and rider. The ocean-racing records of the world abound with classic combinations of skipper and yacht – Paul Hammond and *Nina*, Olin Stephens and *Dorade*, George Martin and Bobby Somerset and *Jolie Brise*, John Illingworth and *Myth of Malham*, David Maw and his *Bluejackets*, Derek Boyer and his anagrams of *Clarion*, Ron Amey and his, Dick Nye and his *Carina*s, Arthur Slater and his *Prospects*, Ted Heath and his *Morning Cloud*s – to name but a few. In this book I have from the outset assumed however that the design of the yacht is the paramount race-winning factor on the further assumption – not entirely unfounded – that designers get the skippers they deserve and vice-versa.

In this book I have attempted to trace the evolution of offshore yacht design from its early history to the present day and to give the reader an understanding of the major factors involved in the process. It is essentially a 'light-displacement' book not settling deeply into the technical waters upon which it floats. I have as far as possible, for example, avoided the use of mathematical formula but I have assumed that those who read this book will have some knowledge already of the elements of sailing theory. Those who prefer a greater depth or heavier scantlings to their knowledge will I am sure find all they require in the bibliography at the end.

Although this book is mostly about offshore racing craft it would not be appreciably different if it dealt with offshore cruising yachts. As with the modern car, today's racing model is tomorrow's touring saloon. There are therefore few cruising yachts which do not owe a great deal to ocean-racing experience for their safety, comfort and ease of handling. The evolution of the one is that of the other.

I have made acknowledgements in the appropriate place but I would wish to express my particular indebtedness to two sources of information used in compiling this book. The first is the Royal Ocean Racing Club in the persons of Mary Pera, Hope Kirkpatrick, Alan Green and W. R. Matthews. The other is that supreme authority on yacht design and all matters relating to it – Douglas Phillips-Birt, AMRINA. He has covered his subject so admirably that it is difficult for us lesser mortals who have sat at his feet for years to say anything that he has not already said and said better.

A.C.H.

Royal Ocean Racing Club
St James's Place
London

Acknowledgements

I would like to thank the following for their help in the preparation of this book:

Anthony Churchill, Editor of *Seahorse* for his permission to use plate numbers 18, 19, 20, 21, 22 and 23 which first appeared in his magazine and also for the use of figures 6 and 18

H. F. Kay and G. T. Foulis & Co Ltd, Henley on Thames, for the use made of diagrams which first appeared in *The Science of Yachts, Wind and Water* – figures 4, 7, 8, 10 and 12

C. A. Marchaj and Adlard Coles Ltd for the use of the diagrams which first appeared in *Sailing Theory and Practice* – figures 9 and 11

Lloyd's Register of Shipping for figure 15

Douglas Phillips-Birt and Adlard Coles Ltd for figure 5 which is based on a diagram in *Sailing Yacht Design* and for extracts from *British Ocean Racing*

Douglas Phillips-Birt and Faber & Faber for brief extracts from *An Eye for a Yacht*

Alfred Loomis and Arno Press for brief extracts from *Ocean Racing 1866-1935*

I
From Work-boat to
Interface Vehicle

In modern scientific terms, because a sailing yacht is neither completely immersed in the sea nor entirely borne in the air but operates along the turbulent margin between the two elements it is by definition an 'interface vehicle'. In another sense, too, it is also an interface vehicle. Its design is neither entirely art nor yet entirely science and again, in design terms, it falls in the turbulent margin between them. In this book we shall be examining the influences which have determined the evolution of yacht design over the last century or so and, in particular, we shall be looking at the quiddity of yachts in general: what makes them what they are. The object is straightforward – to establish at least some of the basic knowledge against which yacht designs can be judged in the latter half of the 1970s. A brief course, if you like, in yacht appreciation.

In the global sense – viewed that is as a whole – the process of the evolution of the modern yacht from the rough working boat of antiquity to its present-day form takes place against a background familiar in many other spheres of human activity from medicine to astronomy. It is the gradual replacement of conventional contemporary wisdom with its undertones of tradition, folklore and sometimes downright superstition by a steadily increasing volume of knowledge based upon scientific observation and mathematically verifiable fact. As it happens, science and mathematics found their way only slowly into yacht design and even now there is a great deal we do not know and more that we cannot adequately quantify. This said, however, the modern educated yachtsman who wishes to be able to appraise and appreciate the finer points of the latest designs will need rather more than the eye for beauty and a taste for curves, which was all his nineteenth-century predecessor required.

There are, of course, a number of ways in which we can judge or 'appreciate' yachts. We can judge then artistically – i.e. 'aesthetically' if that word can be applied to some of the more rugged creations which have appeared in the latter-day offshore world – but this is a very inexact process. It was all very well for the great Will Fife of Fairlie to proclaim of his yachts that 'if it looks right, it is right'. He served a more leisured and less technically exacting age. For good looks in yachts are a matter of contemporary taste and carry with them no guarantee of either success or survival. You do not have to look nice to win races and throughout the 150 years or so of evolutionary process of yacht design, winning races has been the condition for a design to be copied and hence, unlike the dinosaur, to survive. Indeed, as we shall see there have been as many ugly ducklings among the real trend-setters as there have been swans.

We can judge yachts historically – that is by tracing the evolution of design and the influence of tradition. As that truly great writer on yacht design, D. Phillips-Birt, has observed: 'In the acquirement of a good eye for a boat it is, perhaps, impossible to know too much history.' There remains a good deal of truth in the statement and we shall be looking closely at a number of historic yachts throughout this book. The pace of events in the field of yacht design has been such however that during the seventeen years since that statement was written, almost as much technical history has occurred as in the century which preceded it.

In an age of series-production like-seeming yachts, one needs to look rather more closely at technical data than at the boat herself if an adequate judgement of her capabilities is to be made. This process can be carried to great lengths and, with the aid of models, testing tanks and computers, a complete performance envelope for a particular design can probably be predicted. By this method many modern designs are improved. Prediction of this sort does not of itself however produce designs, but it assists in the selection of alternatives. Such methods are however beyond our scope and we shall content ourselves with quantifying the process of comparison as an aid to understanding. As Lord Kelvin, the great physicist and himself no mean sailor, once said:

> When you can measure what you are speaking about and express it in numbers you know something about it; and when you cannot measure it, when you cannot express it in numbers, your knowledge is of a meagre and unsatisfactory kind.

We should begin perhaps by being clear what we mean here by the term 'yacht'. The old dictionary definition of 'a vessel privately owned and used for pleasure' is rather too broad for our purpose for it would cover many boats which are for various reasons only on the fringe of design development either because their development was frozen into one-design class long ago or simply because local craftsmen always 'built 'em that way'. Our business is inevitably with the mainstream of yacht development which means in essence the evolution of the habitable cruiser-racer which is the dominant type of the current age just as the inshore day-racing boat dominated the scene before and after World War I. The eminent British designer, Jack Laurent Giles, once spelled out what was required of a modern design and his definition is very close to our purpose:

> The ability to maintain at sea, in a boat providing accommodation for those on board, the maximum attainable speed and to achieve this is combination with easy handling, easy steering, general mannerliness, dry decks and a comfortable motion.

Though we shall be dealing mainly with keel boats this definition does not exclude the impetus and example already being offered to conventional yacht design by the attractive performances offshore of the growing numbers of multi-hulled sailing craft, or that which has already been made, especially in the design of masts and sails, of the ubiquitous racing dinghy.

Cruising men will perhaps dismiss the requirements for 'the maximum attainable speed' in our definitions as being something necessary only for the racing fraternity. Yet a fast boat is usually a safer boat and easier to handle in a sea-way with a restricted crew. Safer because it is invariably much better to windward than a slower boat and easier to handle because, quite frequently, it requires less canvas to drive it. Speed in yachts may be essential in absolute terms only in racing boats but, like speed in cars and speed in horses, it is the quintessence of the efficiency of the breed. The racing circuit is thus the laboratory of design testing in yachts no less than in other vehicles. In this chapter and throughout this book we shall, therefore, be interested in the pace setters of the sailing scene not necessarily for themselves and their individual racing achievements but for the influence that they exerted on the evolutionary development of the design of offshore sailing craft.

There are comparatively few yachts in the past 150 years or so since yachting began to take on the form in which we know it today which were genuine trend-setters. Yachts, that is, that changed the whole shape of yachts to come. The first I have chosen is the fabulous *America* to give us a starting-point. Inevitably, since yacht development follows the same exponential 'learning curve' common to the development of science as a whole over the same period, there is a long gap in time between *America* and our next example *Jolie Brise* but little in performance. Thereafter, however, as the progress of the curve steepens, time intervals shorten and performance improves by leaps and bounds and we include *Dorade*, the first purpose-built ocean racer seen in British waters, then *Myth of Malham,* author of her own particular brand of post-war revolution, *Carina*, the bell-wether of the dominance of US design in the larger class of cruiser racer. Finally we include *Noreyma VIII*, the first non-American yacht and the first 'production' boat to win the Bermuda Race, as the epitome of the 1970s' offshore glass-fibre, series-built racer. (Fig 1 illustrates the hull shape of each of these yachts.)

Before we examine the shapes, vital statistics and performance of each of these designs any further let us trace in outline the history of the major design development since the middle of last century.

This brings us back to the main theme of this chapter: the rising tide of general scientific knowledge in a host of related fields from pure naval architecture to the production of textiles for sails, carrying with it a burgeoning of improvements in yacht design. But like any tide its progress in amplitude has been neither constant nor regular. As yachting emerged from the workboat era, scientific progress was almost imperceptible and understandably so. Something like 10,000 years of trial-and-error development had gone before and the age of sail, at least in commercial terms, was reaching that plateau of perfection which invariably heralds obsolescence. Despite the superb performance of the sailing clippers, the eclipse of sail by steam was just around the corner. As the very prosperity engendered by an era of the steam-ships created a new demand for leisure activity on the more protected inlets round our coast, more thought, more money and more experimentation was directed towards sailing craft. Not all of it was scientific, sensible or well directed. There was the period of mathematical and mechanical gimmickry which, all too often on the late Victorian era, was mistaken for scientific progress. A typical example was the retrogressive era of the 'plank on edge' in British waters and its contemporary 'skimming dish' era in North American. By World War I, however, genuine scientific development and the applied lessons of the highly competitive inshore racing arena had stabilised hull shapes into something very similar to that which we know today. Progress was being made too in the development of the 'Marconi' mast and the Bermudian rig. But these developments remained for the most part, at least on this side of the Atlantic, confined to the inshore racing fleets, and deep-sea cruising yachts continued to follow the traditional designs of their pilot-cutter, fishermen and quay-punt ancestors. It was to take several years of experience of racing offshore to mould the best features of the offshore cruiser and the inshore racer together to produce the modern cruiser/racer. In this development the role of the rating rule was crucial.

There is little doubt that boat-for-boat modern designs are superior in performance to their predecessors. Of more importance perhaps for our subject here, however, is relative speed – one design against another contemporary design on a boat-for-boat basis such as

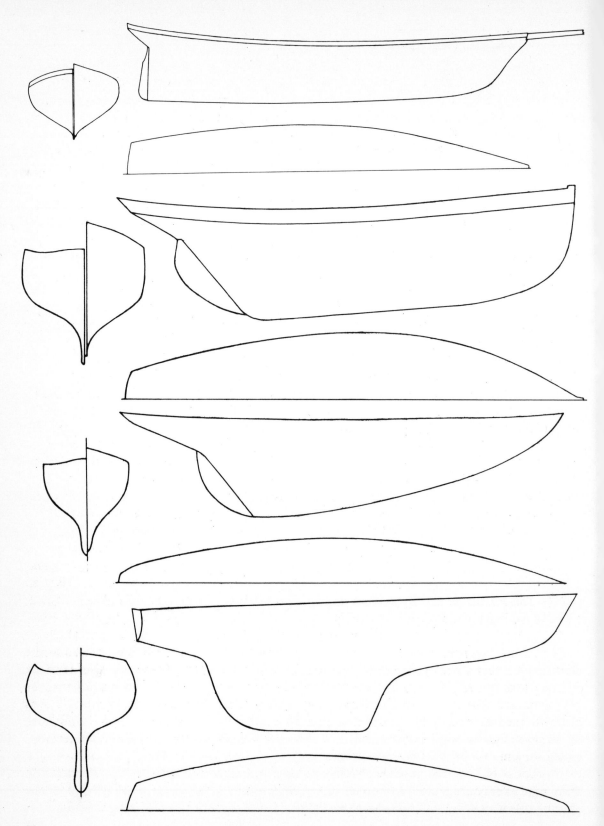

14

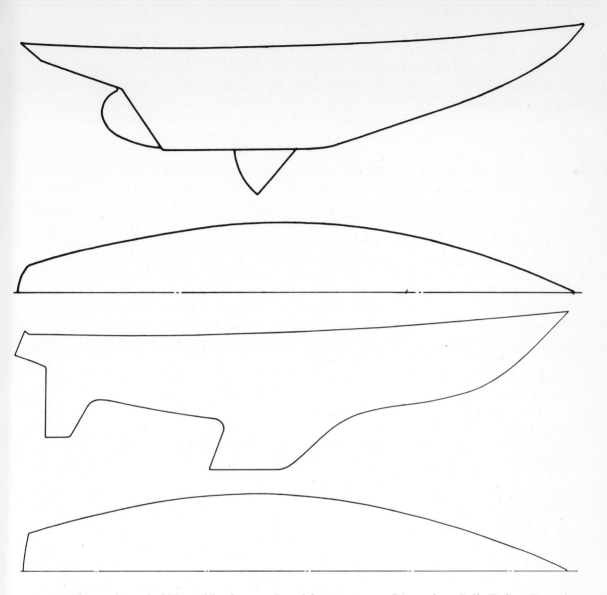

FIG 1 *Sheer plans, half-breadth plans and midship sections of* America, Jolie Brise, Dorade, Myth of Malham, Carina, Noreyma VIII.

we get in one-class (not to be confused with 'one-design class') sailing like the One, Half and Quarter Ton series and speed relative to a rating rule such as we get in the major offshore competitions round the world. To use an analogy from golf, one-class racing might be medal play with both players on the same handicap; racing offshore under the rating rule is match play with the International Offshore Rule supplying bogey for the course.

One-design inshore racing needs no rating rule but, as we have observed already, the establishment of a one-design class freezes that design for evermore. If we are to achieve the twin purpose of allowing yachts of widely different types to race together fairly and at the same time to encourage designers to initiate improvements to hull and rig, we have to devise a rating rule which will strike a reasonable balance between these two requirements. In a later chapter we shall be looking into the evolution of rating rules themselves but for our present historical purpose it is enough perhaps to observe with G. L. Watson, the designer of King Edward VII's immortal *Britannia*: 'Throughout the modern story of yachting the tonnage (i.e. rating) question has been the all-absorbing one.' Watson was writing at the beginning of this century but his words as we shall see are equally true seventy years on – 'rating' rule CCA, RORC, IOR Mark III (our main interest here) is a governing factor in design. For not only has the rating rule of the day throughout the history of yacht development been the 'bogey' – in both senses of that word – for the designer; it has also been to some extent an expression of contemporary technical understanding. From the early days therefore we have seen a pattern of ebb and flow repeated over and over again. Sometimes the design wave has advanced beyond the rating wave, sometimes the rating rule is, as it were, further up the scientific beach. But the pattern is clear enough. First of all owners of yachts of varying sizes and designs wish to race against each other in reasonable equity. Somebody then devises a method of assessing various characteristics of the contenders and comparing them in such a way as to arrive at a handicap system which owners are prepared to accept. (Admittedly with the benefit of hindsight from a more technical age to a lesser, it is nonetheless one of the most remarkable aspects of the story of yacht development that so many tough-minded owners have been prepared to submit for so long to some of the rating rules that were thought up. Such perhaps are the benefits of technical ignorance – and ignorance never spoiled competition.) Yachts then happily compete with each other on the basis of the agreed rule for several seasons. Then quite suddenly there appears on the scene a yacht which is either so technically advanced or so exploits the rating rule – usually both – that it proves virtually unbeatable. Characteristically, such yachts are immediately condemned by the pundits of the day as cheats and upstarts – and invariably too as 'hideous', 'vulgar' and 'offensive to the eye' – but they still go on winning. Since no racing yachtsman will long accept second-place, the intruding upstart is copied and a new design phase is begun. Owners of old outclassed yachts put pressure on the rating authorities to change the rule to eliminate the 'freaks'. The rule is reviewed and since those concerned tend to be (at least in recent years) of more technical bent than the average owner, the better aspects of the intruders tend to be kept in the revised rule and some of the less desirable aspects of the older designs are quietly penalised. The result is that an improved design to meet the rule evolves until, of course, the next 'freak' appears and wins. However, since each time the rule is revised some loophole or other is closed, technical or structural improvements within the confines of the rating rule offer better prospects of success than do rule-beating gimmicks. But close attention to the rule is paramount, for winning margins are extremely narrow. *Noreyma* won the 1972 Bermuda Race by a margin of 24 min of corrected time over three days – about $\frac{1}{2}$ of 1 per cent. And only a shade over 1 per cent separated the first five yachts. In this way, the prospect of anyone driving a real breach through the current IOR rule seems remote but a 1 or 2 per cent gain in individual performance could do it and there is nothing in the history of yacht design which suggests that sooner or later it will not be done.

The first of the 'intruders' is usually accepted to have been the fabulous *America* of America's Cup fame ('Built', they said, 'to represent a nation'). She sailed across the Atlantic – a condition of America's Cup challengers until the World War II and one whose passing has been detrimental to the standing of the race itself and to some extent to yacht development – and hence was 'providing accommodation for those on board' as required by our definition. She was in other words a cruiser/racer. The story of how she eclipsed the best yachts in

British waters is a tale often told and need not be repeated here save for the observation that though the contenders ranged in both size and shape as well as rig, they raced level. Had there been any valid form of rating rule the winner would undoubtedly have been the 'gallant little *Aurora'* (she was only 47 tons displacement compared with *America*'s 147 tons) which finished only 8 min behind. But *America*'s greatest impact was on the design of future yachts. Until her arrival on the British yachting scene, the time-honoured hull shape was a blunt full apple-bow on a long keel with a finely tapered stern – the 'cod's head and mackerel tail' of the Elizabethan era. 'Nature displays herself in forming creatures suitable to their various actions in the several elements.' (The concept of the interface vehicle was still a century or more away.) But *America* changed all that. As a contemporary reporter described her:

> She has a low black hull two noble sticks of extreme rake without an extra rope . . . When close to her you see that her bow is as sharp as a knife . . . a little forward of the mainsail where she has her greatest beam . . . Her stern is remarkable broad, wide and full . . .

But her defeated competitors among the British sailing fraternity had other – more pompous – views: 'She is a mere shell, intended only for racing; *our* yachts are seagoing vessels, safe anywhere.' (The italics are mine.)

America's sails too were revolutionary. British sails at the time were cut very full of loose-woven flax and were invariably loose footed – not laced to the boom. In contrast *America* had sails of close-texture cotton lashed firmly to the boom and pulled as flat as possible. In short, she was a whole technical order of magnitude ahead of her British rivals. She was the prototype of the modern yacht and she was the prototype too of the trend-setter which from time to time over the next hundred years would shatter the complacency of British yachtsmen in demonstrating the seemingly infallible ability of the New World to upset the balance – and self-satisfaction – of the Old.

Another established technical pattern may also have been followed – a British basic idea better developed, better produced and, above all, better advertised by our American cousins. *Mosquito*, built in England in 1848, had many of the characteristics of *America* and it seems at least probable that the latter's designer knew something of the 'scientific' Scott Russell wave-line theory which may have lain behind the idea. Nonetheless, the shape of British yachts began to change as a result of *America*'s successes. Bows became finer and more drawn out, hence the waterlines lengthened whilst displacement changed little. Although it was not fully appreciated why greater length for a given displacement meant greater speed, yachts began to lose proportion and balance as the trend was pursued to its extremes. There followed on this side of the Atlantic, between about 1860 and 1890, the 'plank-on-edge' period we have already mentioned where yachts having more than six beams in a waterline length were not unknown. But these were largely the inshore day racers. The late Victorian era was the heyday of the inshore racing day-boat and the rule-makers in their largely unscientific attempts to eliminate rule-cheating merely served to proliferate freaks of all types as we shall see in chapter 6. The boats produced were not however expected to go seriously to sea or for that matter provide accommodation for the crew. In this respect, as we shall see later, the traditional and normal laboratory function of the race-track was in the longer term to serve the development not only of design but also the improvement of rating and rule-making. Much the same sort of thing happened on the other side of the Atlantic. Whereas the British tradition was heavy displacement and heavily ballasted deep draught on narrow beam, the United States tradition was for light displacement, broad beam and little ballast except the centre-board. Thus in the wild experimental days of the last century, where the British evolved the narrow 'plank-on-edge' type with a 'lead mine' in her keel, the United States evolved the 'skimming dish' relying mainly on beam for stability. Both extremes had occasionally fatal results – capsizes in the U.S. and unexplained founderings in British waters.

Cruising men with their customary caution would have no truck with these dangerous developments inshore and preferred the traditional work-boat type of proven sea-going ability. They either converted workboats themselves or else they had yachts specifically designed in the workboat image. Some fishermen types were chosen but most favoured were the faster sea-kindly cutters like pilot cutters, Falmouth quay-punts and their French and Scandinavian equivalents. These were safe, seaworthy but, by modern standards, slow, especially to windward, and, above all, excellent at 'heaving to' in a seaway. Across the Atlantic however the elegant and highly developed Baltimore schooners, a design already tried and tested in the risks and rivalries of the lucrative trade of opium smuggling, were an almost ready-made cruiser/racer for the growing American offshore yachting fraternity. They were to give the United States an advantage offshore which it continues to enjoy to the present day.

The division between the racing yacht and the cruising yacht was more marked in the United Kingdom than it was in the United States. To some extent the dichotomy was bridged by the need for America's Cup challengers to sail the Atlantic and also by the lessons that successive defeats in that event rammed home to the British. Again we see the race-track laboratory at work for it was in the shape of the English yacht *Thistle* that the extremes of racer and cruiser and plank-on-edge and skimming dish achieved a compromise and design was brought back to a sensible course. But in the United Kingdom, in sharp distinction from the United States, the separation of cruising from offshore racing continued. Whereas cruising yachtsmen in the United States regarded offshore racing as a natural extension of their sport (the Cruising Club of America took control of offshore racing, the Bermuda Race in particular, when it was founded in 1922), the older and experienced Royal Cruising Club – founded in 1880 – declined to organise the early Fastnet races regarding the whole venture as foolhardy and unseamanlike. The establishment of a separate club (now the Royal Ocean Racing Club) was therefore inevitable for progress in yachting like progress in other spheres depends much upon the initiative of the non-conformist. This separation too, which led unavoidably to the development of different and to some extent rival philosophies by men of equal talent and ability, did not help the progress of yacht design in the United Kingdom until the very success of ocean racing brought benefit to both classes.

The first Bermuda Race was held in 1906 and though it attracted an entry of only three starters it was in effect the beginning of the 'open' entry formalised ocean-racing as we know it today. During the nineteenth century there had been a considerable number of Trans-atlantic races mostly in connection with challenges for the America's Cup and thus of a rather restricted and private nature. The yachts taking part too were of a size very different from anything known in the offshore world today outside the Tall Ships Race. The famous *Cambria*, heroine of many a Victorian lithograph still to be found in clubhouses today, was schooner rigged, 108 ft overall and carried thirty-six hands. From this early experience stemmed two developments important to the evolution of the modern offshore yacht. The first was the basic idea that the oceans of the world could be crossed in safety by comparatively small vessels not just as an exercise in survival – the great single-handers like Slocum and Voss had already demonstrated that fact far more effectively – but that the margin between simple survival and sheer suicide was more than adequate to permit yachts to sail competitively. That the margin was narrow was borne out by the experience of yachts like *Fleetwing* in the first of the Transatlantic Races in 1866 which lost no less than six hands overboard in a gale. The second development was less immediate in its impact than the first – the revelation of the inadequacies of the design of hull, sails and gear of contemporary yachts which made the margin of safety so narrow. This is not to suggest that anything was to be done about it for decades – our forbears bore the loss of a few paid hands with cheerful equanimity – but, particularly in the United States, thought began to be given by yacht designers and builders to the problems of sailing a yacht at full speed at sea, if not in complete safety then at least without the tiresome delays created by the need to look for men lost overboard. In essence this meant the gradual eradication of the more menacing aspects of design and rig – low freeboard especially amidships, narrow beam, long fine bows and sterns lacking in buoyancy, 'fidded' topmasts and bowsprits that had to be reefed. The formalisation of offshore racing in the shape of the Bermuda Race and to a lesser extent the Honolulu Race meant that there developed in American waters a new fast type of cruising yacht which had no counterpart in Europe when the first Fastnet was sailed in 1925.

The story of the early Fastnets and the controversy which surrounded them makes fascinating reading in itself but there is little that is immediately relevant to the evolution of design. The entry of the first Fastnet was a reflection of the backward state of the British offshore sailing scene in the mid-1920s. It comprised three pilot cutters (including a Le Havre pilot cutter, *Jolie Brise*, the eventual winner), a fishing-boat type yacht, a Norwegian pilot cutter type, a Dutch ketch and one converted inshore 'plank-on-edge'. They were all proven cruising yachts of heavy displacement, gaff rigged with heavy spurs and laborious gear. The second Fastnet in 1926 saw the first glimmer of change when *Hallowe'en*, a Bermuda-rigged fast cruiser designed by the famous Fife specifically for the Fastnet, came in third despite some difficulty with her much criticised rig. Two years later came the first of the American purpose-designed and built 'real' ocean-racers – *Nina*. She was not, however, a classic rule-beater. The resentment she aroused was not so much caused by her design as by the fact that she was clearly intended to win – an attitude shocking to contemporary opinion in the United Kingdom. The importance of *Nina* is that she was in effect not so much a trend-setter herself – there was much in her design that was true to the Baltimore schooner tradition – but that she heralded the change to come. And come it did in the form of the American yawl *Dorade*, which won the Fastnet Races of 1931 and 1933 by a disturbingly large margin.

Dorade was designed by Olin Stephens and – here again established a trend which extends until today – sailed by his brother Rod. She was the genuine prototype of the modern ocean-racer – masthead rigged with mechanically perfect rigging, powerful winches and a host of labour-saving devices. She completely outclassed her British-designed contemporaries for weatherliness, seakindliness and comfort, and it was not until the appearance of the Fife-designed *Latifa* and the Nicholson *Bloodhound* and the Robert Clark *Benbow* in the years immediately before World War II that British designers were able to begin to produce her like.

Though ocean-racing was impossible throughout World War II, ideas were being developed for the ideal post-war ocean-racer especially in the mind of that greatest of innovators,

Captain John Illingworth. The result was *Myth of Malham* whose design was completed by Jack Laurent Giles.

The *Myth* fully deserved her name, for as long as men go racing offshore she will be recalled as one of the all time greats. She was a superb racing yacht – she won the Channel and Fastnet Races in her first season (1947) and was runner-up in the RORC championship in her last, more than twenty years later. She heralded the arrival of a completely new concept of light-displacement ocean-racer and a new genus of the offshore breed. With her straight sheer, short sawn-off ends, high freeboard and tiny mainsail she was an affront not only to conventional yacht architecture but also to the RORC rating rule of the day. She was the epitome of the classic rule-beater we have discussed before and in many people's eyes she compounded that offence – if offence it be – by being at the same time extremely fast and with better and more spacious accommodation than practically any other yacht then in the fleet. She demonstrated superbly for the first time what have become the dominant features of post-war offshore racing: boats designed from the outset to win, not just to participate, and the supreme importance of massive reserve buoyancy. This latter feature especially – 'no boat in the water and masses of space below deck' – is the key to the next major development in offshore racing: – the evolution of the small ocean-racer.

Before we leave the *Myth* and her impact on the design of offshore yachts we should look briefly at her impact on the RORC rating rule. (We shall be examining the rule itself in more detail in chapter 5.) Two seasons after *Myth*'s dramatic appearance, the RORC rule, through which she had sailed so sublimely, was amended. Some – but not all – of the advantage of snubbed bows and high freeboard was removed but the rule was not restrictive of many of the new features which *Myth* had initiated. It is to the credit of the RORC that no attempt was made to put the clock back. Under the new rule, *Myth of Malham* remained a force to be reckoned with for decades, whilst boats based on her example but less extreme sailed into the winning places. The classic pattern had been followed and the shape of offshore yachts would never be quite the same.

Having demonstrated so effectively that light displacement and a high reserve of buoyancy was a sound and sure winner in ocean-racers on 33 ft waterline, Captain Illingworth turned his attention to the smaller boats, and in 1950 founded the Junior Offshore Group. In doing so he was also laying the foundations of a completely new departure in offshore racing and one which was to enhance immeasurably the popularity and proliferation of the sport. The harbinger here was a remarkable little boat called *Sopranino*, 17·5 ft on the waterline, and designed by Jack Laurent Giles who had given substance to John Illingworth's ideas behind the *Myth*. *Sopranino* in 1950 was precluded by the RORC rule of the day from taking part officially in the 1950 Race to Santander. So she went just for the ride and arrived only one day later than most of the fleet. Later she sailed the Atlantic in $28\frac{1}{2}$ days.

Sopranino was the first of the many and eventually the RORC relented and lowered its LWL limits so that today we have classes down to 21 ft rating, the IOR Mark III covering yachts from 16 ft rating upwards. It was the French, however, in the true 'corsair' tradition, who developed the small offshore racing yacht to a high peak of perfection. They were instrumental too, in 1966, in putting forward the idea that the then virtually moribund One Ton Cup, a trophy first presented in 1899 and competed for first by 'One Tonners' and then IYRU 6 m inshore yachts, should become an offshore event. The initiative came from M. Peytel of the Cercle de la Voile in Paris and races were arranged for yachts racing 'boat-for-boat' with a specified maximum RORC rating – 22 ft. The idea caught on and we now have Two Ton,

Threequarter Ton, Half Ton and Quarter Ton Cup events. The French, as is their just due, have tended to dominate the smaller 'Cups' in recent years.

We left the main ocean-racing stream at *Myth* and her imitators. But *Myth* was a British native champion and, though she did as well as any previous British yacht in the Bermuda, she could not quite lift the prizes in American waters. It was an echo of an old story. Though yachts designed to the RORC rule were capable enough as performers in the absolute sense, they were not winners under the CCA rule. Contrariwise, yachts designed to the CCA Rule soon demonstrated their ability to win under the RORC Rule. We were pretty well back in the situation of the early 1930s that British-designed boats could win their own races only when the Americans weren't present. Robert Clark's *Favona* won the Fastnet in 1953 and then the American designers took over. *Carina*, designed by Phil Rhodes, collected two successive Fastnets, and started the ball rolling – rather, perhaps, the band-wagon – because British and European owners turned to American designers for yachts that would win and they were not disappointed. Sparkman & Stephens – perhaps the greatest name ever in yacht design – claimed (among a host of other battle honours) – the Fastnets in 1959 (the Swedish-owned *Anitra*), 1961 (Dutch-owned *Zwerver*), and 1963 (the British-owned *Clarion of Wight*). In 1965, to drive home the American advantage, a new yacht designed by a new designer, *Rabbit* by R. E. Carter, sailed away with the Fastnet Cup. Two years later the French, with the immortal Tabarly in *Pen Duick III*, claimed the trophy, but, as series-built glass-reinforced plastic yachts became increasingly numerous in the British offshore fleets, American design increasingly predominated. Carter won the Fastnet again in 1969 – the last of the Fastnets sailed under the RORC rating rule – with *Red Rooster*, which was again primarily intended for the CCA racing circuit. The 1971 Fastnet was the first to be sailed under the International Offshore Rule Mark II which was introduced in January 1970. It was won by the Australian-owned *Ragamuffin* – designed once again by the redoubtable Sparkman & Stephens, who also had yachts in the leading places in all the larger classes in the Fastnet and in the RORC Points Championship. The following year – the 'quiet' season of 1972 – Sparkman & Stephens-designed yachts dominated the British offshore scene from the RORC championship in Classes I–IV to the Solent Points Championship and many of the regional offshore championships. The French continued to dominate the smaller classes and it was hard to find a British-designed yacht among the winners. Significantly, too, it was also the year that the great innovator Captain John Illingworth announced his retirement. British design seemed to have touched rock bottom.

A range of Sparkman & Stephens-designed yachts sail in British waters from the famous 'one-offs' like the second *Morning Cloud* (the first *Morning Cloud* was a series-built SS 34) to a range of series-built yachts of which the best-known are the Finnish-built Swans. *Noreyma VIII*, one of the yachts I have used as an example of modern design, is a Swan 48 built by Nautor in Pietsaari in Finland. So, in 1972, we have a British-owned-and-crewed yacht, of American design and Finnish built, winning the principal American offshore race – and some people still argue that the International Offshore Rule was unnecessary!

So much then for the history. What of the present day and the future? Yacht design remains evolutionary in the sense that it remains rather easier and much more certain of success to try and improve the performance of an existing design rather than create something entirely new from scratch. The main role of applied science is in the field of performance prediction either to improve yacht behaviour in general or to predict performance of a particular design. The method calls for either extensive testing of tank models or fully instrumented full-scale yachts followed by the use of high-speed computers to analyse the results. The process is expensive in both time and money and far from certain. A successful design may be analysed and its good points retained whilst its bad points are reduced or eliminated. But there can be no guarantees that the revised design will necessarily perform better in competition. As ever, the criterion for the survival of a design is the ability to outsail other boats.

But what about comparative performance in the historical sense? Are the yachts of today really so superior in speed, windward ability and sea-keeping qualities than those of the past?

Let us look first at speed. Although inshore it is possible to measure the speed of yachts against measured distances (V_s), the basis of speed measurement offshore is 'round trip speed,' (V_0). This is the actual elapsed time taken over a specific rhumb line distance offshore which is likely to have involved all points of sailing and the usual vicissitudes of the open sea from calm to gale. For comparison purposes, one would generally look for an 'out and back' trip like the Fastnet or a series of offshore events during the same season rather than a 'downhill' dash across the Pacific or the Atlantic. Historically, however, there is not a great deal of data to work from and it is thus impossible always to choose the most suitable. We are also, of course, comparing yachts of a widely differing size and hence mere knots of forward speed are largely meaningless unless we take size into account. Here the basic measure is the 'speed length ratio'. We shall see in the next chapter that because a hull has to push aside a train of surface water waves, the length of the hull governs the length of the wave system and this in turn governs the speed. The relationship is known as the 'Vee over root L' ($V/L^{\frac{1}{2}}$) and makes it possible to compare the speeds of hulls of different lengths. It forms the basis of Froude's 'Law of Comparison' which he enunciated in 1876 and which was one of the major scientific achievements in the field of naval architecture in the nineteenth century. We shall examine the speed/length relationship in greater detail in the next chapter but in general terms it means that a 36 ft LWL yacht at 6 knots ($V/L^{\frac{1}{2}} = 1 \cdot 0$) and a 25 ft LWL at 5 knots are performing at an equivalent speed. In other words, speed/length ratio is the 'Mach' number of the sea. With displacement hulls, the maximum speed under full press of sail is about $V/L^{\frac{1}{2}} = 1 \cdot 6$ but $1 \cdot 5$ is rarely exceeded for long. On the wind, speeds in excess of $V/L^{\frac{1}{2}} = 1 \cdot 0$ are rare. The yacht *America* crossed the Atlantic in 21 days to collect the cup which bears her name. This is $V/L^{\frac{1}{2}} = 0 \cdot 59$. In 1866, *Henrietta* sailed from Sandy Hook to the Needles in thirteen days – $V/L^{\frac{1}{2}} = 0 \cdot 96$ – a very fast passage. Going the other way – mostly to windward – *Cambria* took twenty-three days – $V/L^{\frac{1}{2}} = 0 \cdot 51$. *Nina* crossed in 1928 at $0 \cdot 74$ and *Dorade* in 1931 at $0 \cdot 96$ both west to east. This speed was not bettered until 1950 when Adlard Coles in *Cohoe* crossed at a speed ratio of $1 \cdot 05$. In 1952, Errol Bruce, in the 24 ft LWL *Samuel Pepys* turned in a speed of $V/L^{\frac{1}{2}} = 1 \cdot 05$. Ten years later the 58 ft *Ondine* won the 1963 Transatlantic Race with a speed ratio of $0 \cdot 89$. In 1972, *Noreyma* sailed back from her Bermuda Cup win, from Bermuda to Bayona in Spain, in twenty days – the equivalent of $0 \cdot 89$. In other words, when it comes to sailing downhill across oceans, there is apparently little to choose in performance between the latest yachts and those of an earlier age. Can this really be true? The short answer is that whilst speeds (or speed ratios) have altered little, the size of yacht and the amount of sail required for equivalent performances off the wind have changed dramatically. Also, as we shall see in the next chapter, LWL is not always a measure of effective sailing length. We have also, of course, been dealing with straight crossings of the Atlantic rather than 'round trips'. If we go back to the revival of ocean-racing in British waters just after

World War II, and look at the performance of the class champions in their best races in each Fastnet year, we get a slightly more encouraging picture. The graph at Fig 2 shows the average round-trip speeds (V_0) and the rolling average which rises from 0·85 in 1951 to 0·90 in 1971 – an improvement of only 6 per cent. Even though the figures can make no allowance for the conditions of each season – though there is curiously little indication that 1957, for example, was a 'classic' Fastnet – one might have looked for a more marked improvement than that shown. The key is almost certainly performance to windward. It is worth remembering that even if a yacht can point up to 40° of the true wind, it will still spend well over half of the time close-hauled, and the less well it points, the higher proportion of the round trip time is spent close-hauled. It is worth remembering here that when close-hauled the effective rhumb line distance increases as the secant of the wind-angle made good – 40° means an extra 41 miles in a hundred; 50° means an extra 56, and 60°, twice as far to sail. As we can only expect to sail at forward speeds on the wind of about two-thirds of those attainable sailing free, my suggestion that we spend half the time on the wind is probably on the generous

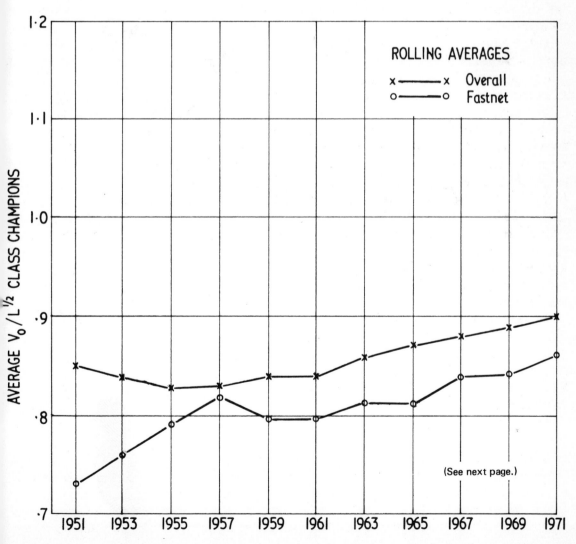

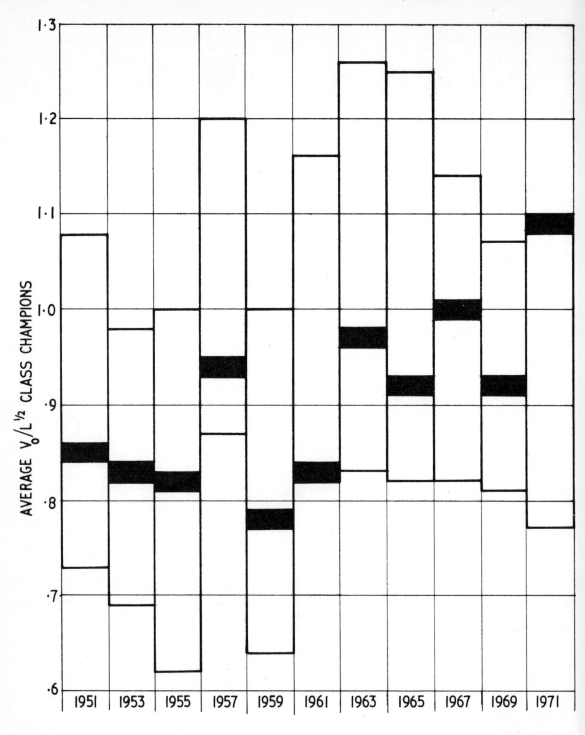

Pillars show range of speeds
Blocks show seasonal average

FIG 2 *Round-trip speeds* (RORC *seasons 1951-71*). *Graph illustrating the average round-trip speeds achieved by the class champions in their best races for the Fastnet seasons 1951–71.*

The British yacht Mosquito, *built in 1848 and designed in accordance with the Scott Russell wave-line theory which called for long hollow-lined bows and short full stern. It is usually accepted that George Steers, the designer of* America, *was guided by the same theory.* Mosquito *was also evolutionary because she was built of iron and had fixed ballast in her keel. She survived into the twentieth century.*

Top: America, *the ship which spawned a thousand facsimiles. Compared with the bluff bowed 'cod's head and mackerel tail' shape of British yachts of her day, she was a revolution. Her angle of entrance at the waterline was only 17°; her greatest beam was well aft of amidships and her short after body is apparent. After her famous cup victory she was beaten in the Queen's Cup at Ryde in 1852 by, among others, her progenitor Mosquito. Bottom:the lines of America. Apart from her length, which resulted from the drawing out of the bows, she was a superbly balanced hull with perfect harmony between her fore and after bodies. She could be sailed with one finger on the tiller, it is said, even in a stiff breeze and a short chop.*

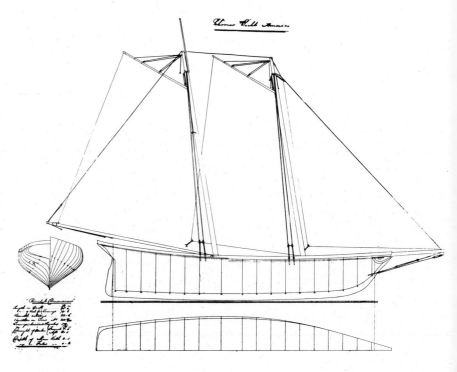

side. As we have already seen, the relative speed ratios off the wind have not changed significantly over the years so it seems probable that the comparatively small average gain in performance is actually in speed made good to windward (V_{mg}). A gain in round trip performance of the order of $V/L^{\frac{1}{2}} = 0.05$ probably represents an improvement on performance to windward of the order of 4° in angle to the true wind *or* 0.15 in forward speed – about 0.75 knots in a 25 ft yacht. It is most likely that the improvement in windward performance lies between these two values with a slight improvement in both.

Absolute values for windward performance are very hard to obtain. There are few records available and where they do exist they frequently depend upon the rather inadequate instrumentation available to our forbears. The following, however, may serve to illustrate the general trend over the years since offshore racing became an established sport. They use the expression 'speed-made-good-to-windward/length ratio' which is nothing more menacing than the speed/length ratio we have already met using V_{mg} for V_s. (The formula is $V_s \cos \gamma/L^{\frac{1}{2}}$.) These values will, of course, also vary with the strength of the wind.

With each type – roughly corresponding to those embodied in *America, Jolie Brise, Dorade, Myth of Malham* and the Sparkman & Stephens series epitomised by *Noreyma*

Type of yacht	Angle to true wind	Speed length ratio	Windward speed ratio
Gaff Rigged Schooner Low aspect ratio sails Low aspect ratio keel Low ballast ratio Rough hull surface	55°	0·40 to 0·60	0·23 to 0·34
Gaff Rigged Pilot Cutter Low aspect ratio sails Low aspect ratio keel Low ballast ratio Rough hull surface	50–55°	0·40 to 0·60	0·23 to 0·38
Bermuda Rigged Schooner Higher aspect ratio sails More effective keel surface External ballast Smoother anti-fouling finish	50°	0·50 to 0·70	0·32 to 0·45
Bermuda Rigged Light Displacement Cutter or Sloop High aspect ratio sails Prounounced high aspect ratio keel High ballast ratio High surface finish High freeboard	45°	0·70 to 1·0	0·50 to 0·70
Bermuda Rigged 'One-off' Ocean Racer Optimum aspect ratio rig – terylene sails Fin keel skeg rudder High ballast ratio Optimum length/beam ratio High freeboard	38–43°	0·70 to 1·1	0·52 to 0·87

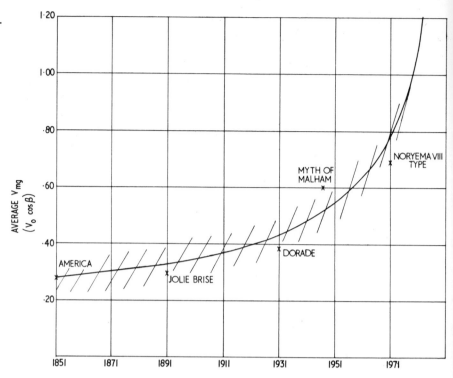

FIG 3 *Graph showing relative improvement in windward speed ratio.*

VIII – I have summarised some of the characteristics of each design. In later chapters of this book we shall be looking into how each of these characteristics exercises its influence upon performance. Before leaving the question of windward performance, a glance at Fig 3 will show how windward speed/length ratio appears to have improved over the years. It suggests that we are now approaching the upper limit and that improvements in windward ability will be increasingly difficult to obtain in future. If we are therefore to continue with progress in yacht performance we may well have to look to other points of sailing to bring this about. We shall be examining this aspect of the design problem in the last chapter.

If the history of windward performance is a rather uncharted area of the ocean of yacht design, that of sea-going ability is delineated by rather more positive soundings. The best known of these is the Beaufort Scale, the well-known scale of numbers for recording the velocity of the wind at sea which was invented by Admiral Sir Francis Beaufort in 1805. Relevant here are the criteria given for action by fishing smacks for the higher wind strengths:

Force 5   'Smacks shorten sail'
Force 6   'Smacks double reef gaff mainsails'
Force 7   'Smacks remain in harbour or lie-to at sea'
Force 8   'Smacks take shelter'

For the modern strongly built, rigged and, above all, strongly crewed ocean-racing yacht, shortening sail probably does not become necessary until well into Force Six and most yachts will continue to go to windward up to about Force Nine. Heaving-to or lying-to at sea anchor is not much practised nowadays but it was done by some yachts in the 1972 Bermuda Race when the wind reached Beaufort Force Ten (55 knots). Nonetheless, the old Beaufort criteria remains a sound guide for the family cruiser!

2

The Way of a Yacht in the Sea

At the beginning of this book I defined a yacht in modern terms as being an 'interface vehicle' because it operated partly in the sea and partly in the air and was not completely immersed in either medium. Looked at in the same way, a yacht can broadly be defined as a device whereby an aerofoil (a sail) and a hydrofoil (a keel) achieve an exchange of momentum between two fluid streams. Of course, the hull and the keel are neither completely immersed in the water nor are the masts and sails freely borne in the air. The mere fact that the yacht is operating along a 'free surface' between two media of different physical characteristics brings problems in its train, as we shall see. For the purpose of the present chapter, however, we shall separate the hull from the mast and the sails and we shall look at the behaviour of the yacht-hull in the water and seek to establish what factors of hull shape and design govern performance. In the next chapter we shall examine how aerodynamic factors affect the performance of the sails. Before however we dismast our imaginary yacht, let us just remind ourselves of the theoretical background to the whole magical process of sailing.

True sailing as distinct from drifting with the wind really only begins when a sailing craft starts to make some progress to windward and the sails and the hull both generate a degree of lift. Optimum values for lift both from the sails and the hull are achieved when the yacht attains its optimum course to windward (that is V_{mg} from chapter 1). Fig 4 shows the forces acting on an upright yacht sailing close-hauled. There are, as you will see, two principal horizontal forces: first, a resultant force from the wind (R_A) and second, one resulting from the water (R_W). Assuming that the boat is sailing at a steady speed then the total (resultant) wind force and the total (resultant) water force must be equal in magnitude and opposite in direction. Breaking these forces down into their components (as is done in Fig 4) we have, for each, two forces at right angles to each other. R_A can be divided into the lift force L_A and, at right angles to it, the drag force, D_A. The angle between L_A and R_A marked in the diagram as ε is known as the wind drag angle. In the case of water forces, the force R_W is the resultant of L_W which is the water lift-force or the force which prevents the boat moving to leeward and D_W which is the water drag force. The angle between L_W and R_W (δ) is the water drag angle. By adding up the angles in Fig 4, it can be seen that β, the apparent wind course angle, is equal to the sum of the two drag angles, i.e. $β = δ + ε$.

There is one other angle which we should mention, and that is the angle between the centre line of the yacht (its heading) and the path through the water which it actually makes good. This is known as the leeway angle and by convention is denoted by the Greek letter lambda (λ). To achieve our greatest velocity through the water it is clear from Fig 4 that we need to achieve the *maximum* resultant sail force and the *minimum* drag angle from the sails coupled with the *minimum* hull drag which in turn will depend upon the hull lift required to maintain course. Also, from our small equation above, if we are to obtain the smallest possible angle to the wind, we need the air-drag angle and the water-drag angle to be as small

FIG 4 *Basic sailing diagram.*

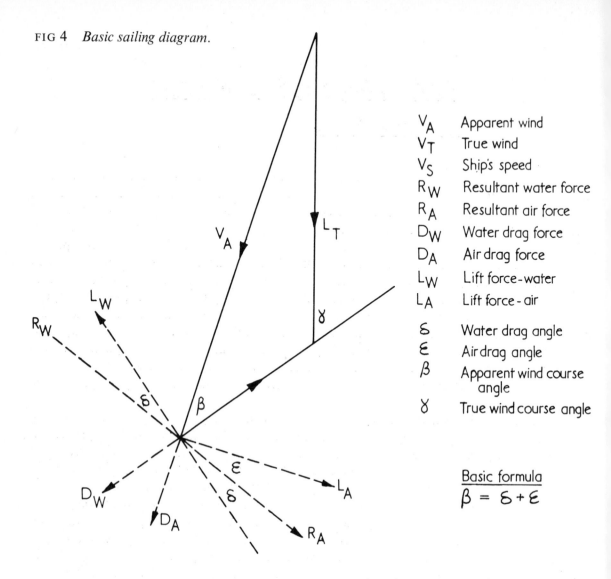

V_A	Apparent wind
V_T	True wind
V_S	Ship's speed
R_W	Resultant water force
R_A	Resultant air force
D_W	Water drag force
D_A	Air drag force
L_W	Lift force-water
L_A	Lift force - air
δ	Water drag angle
ε	Air drag angle
β	Apparent wind course angle
γ	True wind course angle

Basic formula

$$\beta = \delta + \varepsilon$$

as possible. The need for a large resultant force and a small drag angle for both sail and hull holds good for all points of sailing except the dead run when the main criteria are the maximum drag from the sails and the minimum drag from the hull. At all points of sailing, hull drag is thus something which we could well do without, and whilst there is no hope of eliminating drag entirely, the yacht most likely to succeed, other things being equal, will be that which is shaped to produce the minimum hull drag in those conditions of sailing which it is most likely to encounter or for which it is specifically designed. This latter qualification is immensely important. To a large extent, the designer in shaping a hull can optimise the drag characteristics to meet specific conditions. On one extreme, for example, a yacht intended for the Transpacific Race, which tends to be a heavy-air off-wind race, would be shaped to have minimum hull drag at high speed/length ratios. On the other hand, one designed for, say, the One Ton Cup series would almost certainly require to achieve minimum hull drag when close-hauled. The corollary is also true, of course. In selecting optimum conditions one has to accept below-peak performance when those conditions do not obtain and, inevitably, the tendency is to compromise. It is an axiom that extremes in design only win in extreme conditions and extreme conditions are mercifully rare. Nonetheless, within the requirements of compromise there is an infinity of choice.

In the last chapter we saw how in broad terms the shapes of yachts have changed over the last century or so and we had a glimpse of some of the factors which produced these changes. In Fig 1 we have a pictorial representation of those changes and in Figs 2 and 3 a broad estimate of the overall improvement in performance which went with them. We shall now be looking in much closer detail at each of the individual characteristics which determine the shape of a yacht – length, beam, draft, depth, freeboard, displacement, sail area, and the other variables which contribute. Since these characteristics are variable and since they are interdependent – one cannot be altered without affecting the others – we shall be examining too, the relationship between them. In our brief glimpse at comparative performance in Fig 2, we saw something of the relationship in certain circumstances between length and speed. Let us now look much more closely at this all-important quality of length.

It goes almost without saying that the main determinant of a yacht's size is her length. Length over all (LOA) or load waterline length (LWL) is the major factor in determining beam, depth, draft and displacement – all the vital statistics of hull shape. Length, as we have seen, also has a major bearing on performance. But like so many things in the ways of yachts, 'length' itself is an imprecise term and much depends on the way and the circumstances in which it is measured. Let us look first at LOA. In earlier times, LOA was measured between the 'extremities of the hull whether these resulted from hull or rigging' – in other words, bowsprits and bumpkins were included. There is some merit in this procedure because one function of the extra length provided is to supply a base for the rig, and hence permit – other things being equal – a larger sail area for a shorter mast. With our better understanding of sail area aspect ratios nowadays, and our superior methods of mast construction, we have come largely to ignore both the bowsprit and the bumpkin (and not without some gain in safe handling in a seaway as well) in favour of an all-inboard rig. One problem we are faced with however is in comparing LOA over an historic period as we are attempting to do in this book. Records supplying LOA do not always specify how it was obtained but as far as can be verified the LOA used in this book will be in accordance with the modern definition from the International Offshore Rule that LOA is measured 'to include the whole hull but not spars and projections'. LOA is also a main constituent in determining two well-known measures of yacht size – Thames Tonnage and Lloyd's Register Tonnage. It is useful to include them here under the discussion of the relationship of length to size because all too often there is a tendency for the uninitiated to confuse one with the other and both with displacement (W) which is also often measured in tons – in this case, real tons – tons weight. (There is, however, a helpful modern tendency to express both displacement and ballast in pounds.) 'Displacement' means what it says. It is simply the volume of water which a vessel would displace from a tank or a lock if it were lowered into it. As a value, therefore, displacement can be expressed in two ways – either as a measure of volume in cubic feet or as a measure of weight. To convert one to the other, all you need to know is that a cubic foot of salt water weighs 64 lb or there are 35 ft³ of salt water to the ton. Fresh water is less dense at 63 lb/ft³. The usual symbol for displacement as weight is 'W' or a small triangle apex upwards. For volume, 'V' or a small triangle base upwards is used. In this book we shall use W and V.

We shall be looking at Thames Tonnage later when we consider the evolution of rating rules but it provides nowadays a useful comparator of general hull size and it is in that capacity that it largely owes its survival. The basic formula is

$$\frac{(L-B) \times B \times \frac{1}{2}B}{94} = \begin{array}{l} \text{Thames Measurement Tons} \\ \text{(rounded to the nearest ton)} \end{array}$$

L here means virtually LOA and is measured from the fore side of the stem at deck level to the after side of the stern post at deck level. (There are various rules for measuring L when there is no stern post.) B means B_{max} – i.e. the extreme breadth of the hull excluding protrusions. (This method of measurement does not apply to multihulls.)

Thames Measurement clearly places undue emphasis on beam and it was this aspect that led to its eventual eclipse as a rating rule for racing purposes. Nonetheless it has been in use for the best part of a century in one form and another and despite its inaccuracies it provides a common basis for comparison purposes. It has therefore some value for judging the size of one yacht against another in broad terms (say a 'Five Tonner' with a 'Twenty Tonner'), but its limits must be appreciated. It will not differentiate in any observable way between a 'Ten Tonner' and a 'Twelve Tonner' – indeed the former can easily be the bigger boat. It is also, incidentally, the basis upon which, traditionally, yacht builders make their charges – so many pounds sterling per Ton Thames.

The charges for harbour dues and surveys on the other hand are based on registered tonnage and this depends on the laws of the country from which the yacht originates. Generally, however, some method of assessing cargo-carrying capacity is adopted and, in the United Kingdom, this is stamped on the appropriate deck beams. 'Gross register tons' means the total usable space; 'net register tons' means that space less steering space etc, needed for working the ship. The important thing to remember is that neither register tonnage nor Thames Tonnage have any relation to weight or to displacement. Just to add to the confusion, there has emerged since 1965 a class of offshore racing yachts known as 'One Tonners', 'Half Tonners' and 'Quarter Tonners'. The origin of the 'Ton' here is historic and is not related to any specific 'tonnage' measurement other than the IOR where quite arbitrarily, 27·5 ft was the rating chosen for the One Ton Cup. (See chapter 5 for its derivation.)

To clarify all these various measurements, here is an example of the same boat measured under each of the systems:

> *Kealoha* is a 'One Ton Cup' design, i.e. a 'One Tonner';
> she is 13 Tons Thames
>   10·08 Gross register tons; 9·78 net register tons.
> She *displaces* 6·25 tons.

Load waterline length is for performance purposes more significant than LOA but it too is far from being a finite quantity. A designer decides upon a waterline length for his design – design waterline length (DWL) – but is well aware that in the finished yacht the actual waterline length will only approximate to this figure. Hull loading and trim may easily affect LWL even at moorings and when sailing there are a host of dynamic factors of which heel, pitch and wave-making are the main ones, which means that a yacht rarely sails exactly to her designed waterline length. For that matter, even if it were possible to measure LWL on the water within reasonable accuracy, this would be a length applicable only to those particular static and untypical conditions. Although therefore we continue to use LWL as a basis for comparison, what we are really doing is to use this fixed value for a variable value which we might call 'effective sailing length'. This again will vary with conditions and hull shape. Apart from the 'planing' condition where there is an element of dynamic lift to raise the bows, 'effective sailing length' for all practical purposes will lie between LWL and LOA. Hence a useful but rough comparator of probable effective sailing lengths is the relationship, in percentage terms, of LOA minus LWL or, if you like, the overhang component (OC) which can be divided again into 'after overhang component' (AOC) and 'forward overhang component' (FOC). As we shall see, attempts to predict a yacht's 'effective sailing length' is one of the main functions of the rating rules and we shall meet AOC and FOC again in chapter 5. Many modern rating rules have used successfully the artificial but workable device of measuring length as 'length between girth stations' where girth stations are determined by the relationship of 'girth' length to beam. This system has been preserved in the latest rating rule, IOR Mark III.

We have now to consider the crucial relationship between 'length' and sailing speed. First, let us consider further the derivation of the relationship of 'Vee-over-Root L' that we met briefly in the last chapter. As anyone who has ever cast a stone into calm water is aware, the energy of the impact on the water surface is dissipated in the form of radiating waves. Now it just happens that the speed of these waves is governed by their length from crest to crest and is proportional to the square root of this length. The actual relationship is $V = 1{\cdot}34/L^{\frac{1}{2}}$. Thus, as a yacht sails through the water slowly gathering way, the interval between each successive wave – or wave length – she creates will at first be small whilst her speed is low. This means there will be a number of waves along her waterline length – as many as six for example at speeds of around $V/L^{\frac{1}{2}} = 0{\cdot}547$ (say about $2\frac{1}{2}$ knots in a 24 ft LWL yacht). As her speed increases, the number of waves decreases until, at speed/length ratio of $1{\cdot}34$, the wave system is as long as the ship herself, regardless of the ship's size. There is a mounting crest under bow and the counter and a deep hollow amidships usually showing a fair expanse of boot-topping. It is an exciting point of sailing and usually only achieved on a broad reach in a stiff breeze with a lot of sail up. Quite often, too, the pressure of the stern wave is enough force water in through the cockpit drains and a wet cockpit sole is frequently an indication that $V/L^{\frac{1}{2}} = 1{\cdot}34$ has been achieved.

This relationship between speed and length has two other important facets. First, observations made by the British founder of modern naval architecture, William Froude, about 1872, revealed that the wave patterns created by both models and full-size vessels of the same proportions and shape were identical when their speeds were in the proportion of the square roots of their lengths. This means that a 4 ft model being towed in a tank at 2 knots will produce an identical wave pattern to that produced by a real 100 ft ship whose shape is based on the tank model at 10 knots. Furthermore – and this is the important second point – their resistance will be exactly the same per ton of displacement. If we divide the wave-making resistance of the ship and the model by their respective displacements, the answer will be the same for both.

As the $V/L^{\frac{1}{2}}$ ratio approaches $1{\cdot}34$ – sometimes known as the 'theoretical maximum' – the curve of resistance rises steeply because, in effect, the yacht is trying to climb up over its own bow wave. For displacement yachts – that is those which are incapable of planing in any form – the wave-making drag is roughly proportionate to the square of the speed up to about $V/L^{\frac{1}{2}} = 1{\cdot}2$, gradually extending to cube and fourth powers of V_s and above as speed is increased. The effect of this is to put a practical upper limit upon a displacement yacht's speed of about $V/L^{\frac{1}{2}} = 1{\cdot}5$. Even this value is not sustained for long and exceeded for only brief periods when there is likely to have been an element of wave-riding present as well. It is also important to remember that in the conditions of high speed/length ratios with large waves at bow and stern, the effective sailing length will exceed the actual designed waterline length by a significant margin. In these circumstances it is as likely that the effective sailing length of a 24 ft waterline yacht doing, say, 8 knots or $V/L^{\frac{1}{2}} = 1\cdot64$, has become 28 ft (i.e. $V/L^{\frac{1}{2}} = 1\cdot5$) as that the higher speed/length ratio has been attained. This example serves once again to demonstrate the importance not only of a yacht's length to the speed she can achieve but also of the difficulty of determining that length. We shall be looking further into the problem of predicting effective sailing length when we come to the chapter on the rating rule.

But a yacht, of course, is not just a 'length'. It has body in the form of its hull and at a breadth and depth which together delineate its size and weight and hence its displacement. We saw what 'displacement' meant earlier in this chapter in the static sense – i.e. W or V. 'Displacement' is also what it says in the dynamic sense – the yacht has to displace its own weight of water continuously as it sails along. Thus, though we saw earlier that when yachts of widely differing sizes are sailing at the same speed/length ratio their resistance per ton of displacement is the same, we must remember that displacement is a measure of volume and that if we double the size of a yacht by scaling it up all round, the displacement will increase by the cube of the increase in scale, i.e. 8 times. In other words, we can express Froude's famous 'Law of Comparison' in which he determined in 1876 that the resistance due to wave-making of geometrically similar ships varies as the cube of the scale when speeds vary as the square root of the scale. The significance here is that if we increase the scale of a yacht to twice the size of a model, when both are sailing at the same speed/length ratio, the total resistance of the bigger yacht will be, in proportion to her displacement, eight times that of the smaller. This fact becomes important when we come to consider that fundamental factor governing the performance of any machine – 'power to weight ratio' or, in the case of yachts, sail area to displacement.

First, however, let us look rather more closely at the whole question of resistance. If we look at a boat sailing upright downwind, the total resistance is composed of two main elements. The first of these is skin-friction, which is approximately in proportion to the wetted surface of the hull and the 'residual' resistance which is the wave-making resistance we have already discussed, together with form or eddy-making drag. When the yacht heels or goes to windward, two other forms of drag arise – heel drag and side-force – or induced – drag. We shall be looking at these later.

At speed/length ratios of about $1\cdot1$, resistance due to skin-friction and to wave-making are about equal. At lower speed ratios, the greater part of the total resistance is due to skin-friction and as speeds increase above $1\cdot1$, wave-making accounts for an ever-increasing proportion of the total. The following table is an indication of the likely proportions for a 25 ft LWL light displacement yacht:

| Speed (knots) | $V/L^{\frac{1}{2}}$ | Proportion of total resistance | |
		Skin-friction (%)	Wave-making (%)
2·0	0·4	79	21
3·0	0·6	77	23
4·0	0·8	75	25
5·0	1·0	65	35
6·0	1·2	37	63
7·0	1·4	17	83

A point to be made here, of course, is that resistance from both causes is increasing as the yacht goes faster but that wave-making resistance increases more rapidly at the higher speeds. As we saw in chapter 1, the greater proportion of our sailing time is spent at the slower speed/length ratios and that even getting to windward well in a fresh breeze rarely exceeds $V/L^{\frac{1}{2}} = 1\cdot0$. Looking at the preceding table the importance of skin-friction in determining hull-resistance and hence probable performances is obvious.

Skin-friction depends upon four factors: the area of wetted surface; the length of that surface; its roughness; and the speed of the flow over the surface. For a given volume of displacement, the minimum wetted surface would be obtained if it were enclosed in a sphere or – if you remember your Pythagoras – the curved area of a cylinder into which the sphere will just fit. The maximum – for comparison purposes – would be to contain it in a narrow plank. Thus in the days of the older full-bodied yachts – like *America*, for example – the proportion of displacement to wetted surface was lower than it is today with hollow midship sections and deep fin keels. Likewise, given a similar hull profile, a light displacement yacht will have relatively more wetted surface than a heavy displacement yacht of similar size (and, of course, less sail area). But once again, length plays its part. A long yacht experiences less frictional resistance per square foot of wetted surface than does a shorter one assuming that both have surfaces of equivalent smoothness. Assuming too that they are not sailing at the very low speeds when 'laminar' flow conditions may obtain. In these conditions, when the flow of water over immersed parts of the hull remains 'undisturbed' the water flows in 'layers' in contrast with 'turbulent' flow when layer-disturbing eddies are produced – frictional resistance can be of the order of ten times less. Since smaller yachts tend to operate closer to the critical conditions which produce laminar flow this can mean that considerable areas of their underwater surfaces can be offering exceedingly low drag. Again, however, the fundamental smoothness of the yacht's surface plays a crucial part. Some years ago I skippered a remarkable little yacht designed by Illingworth & Primrose called *Blue Charm*. (She was a cold-moulded plywood hull by Wilf Souter of Cowes.) She was outstanding in 'ghosting' conditions in a smooth sea and more than once sailed blithely through the rest of the RORC fleet at 3 knots whilst they were stationary or kedged. On one occasion in a drifting match she finished so far ahead of the rest of the entire fleet that race officials conducted a special enquiry to satisfy themselves that she had actually completed the course. Yet, although a number of hulls were built from the original *Blue Charm* mould and were believed to be identical to her in every respect – indeed some out-performed her in strong winds – none possessed quite her ability in very light airs. The only logical explanation was the achievement of significant areas of 'laminar flow' over her underbody and this achievement was, as Angus Primrose himself would admit, more by accident than design. Yet it is in this direction that there can be a major improvement in yacht performance, and when we consider the shape of yachts to come in a later chapter, we shall be looking at ideas on how skin-drag might be reduced.

But *Blue Charm* too demonstrated the statement I made earlier that at speeds above the critical laminar flow condition, longer yachts have less frictional resistance per square foot of wetted surface than do smaller ones. She was very much a light displacement yacht and, among other things, this means she was something of a sounding board for sea and rigging noises. She also had a comparatively high wetted surface for her displacement. As long as she hissed along she would gain – the laminar flow condition; but as soon as she started to chuckle and her rigging began to sing – events which usually occurred about the same time – the larger boats gradually began to creep up and overtake.

As we are concerned here mostly with comparing one yacht with another, there is no need to go into the deep theory of the effects of the smoothness of the surface of the hull. Provided adequate modern paints are used, there is little to choose as far as smoothness goes between contemporary methods of construction. When it was first introduced, many people thought that GRP (Glass Reinforced Plastic) was inherently smoother and resistant to fouling than was wood. Both these beliefs have now been seen to be largely fallacious. It is the final painting and polish and general maintenance of the finished surface which counts. When, however, we compare yachts historically, going back even to the late 1850s puts us into a different order of surface drag régimes and the further back we go the rougher becomes the original finish and the less effective the anti-fouling measures. When we compare performances, and particularly performance to windward, which, of course, means speeds of $V/L^{\frac{1}{2}}$ of unity or less, the state of bottoms and barnacles is a major factor to be borne in mind.

So far in our consideration of hull resistance, we have not taken actual hull shape into account. By hull shape what is meant, of course, is how the displacement is distributed along the length of the hull. We can look at shape from three points of view: the fore and aft shape; the profile or sheer plan; and the body plan or cross-section in which the main determinant is the midship section.

The midship section is the master section and we will deal with that first because it largely determines the main characteristics of the yacht. Curiously enough, it is not something easily seen nowadays without having a glimpse of the lines plan or seeing a yacht suspended in slings. Most publications will print sail plans, sheer-plans or profiles and deck plans but it is becoming increasingly rare to find a midship section illustrated. At one time it was fashionable for designers to keep the designed displacement of their yachts a secret because W is the key to so many other values in a design. Nowadays lines tend to be kept close to the chest. (Sparkman & Stephens for instance never publish their lines plans.) Competition begins on the drawing board. And the key to any hull design is the midships section.

Earlier in this chapter, when discussing displacement and wetted surface, I pointed out that the minimum wetted surface came from a cylinder. A semicircular section is thus a midship section which would give the minimum wetted surface for a given displacement. The other basic sections are triangular and rectangular. Whilst we do not ordinarily see any of these in pure form – even the Greater London Council garbage barges have the corners of their otherwise rectangular sections rounded off – all midship sections are variants of one or other of the basic forms – frequently a compromise between triangle and semi-circle.

At Fig 5 is a selection of typical midship sections. The first is that of a 'plank-on-edge' and I include it for its historical interest and to show what is meant by heavy displacement and low freeboard. In a seaway the yacht whose section I have illustrated would have been like a half-tide rock. It does bring out other points concerning midship sections as a whole. First, look at the beam/depth ratio and the lack of bilges and absence of garboards. You will then understand why yachts of this type required a lead mine in their keels to have any stability at all. Even then one of them (*Oona*) was lost with all hands – including, deservedly. her designer. Such is the influence of the rating rule of the day!

The second section is that of *America* which is almost triangular with a hard, high bilge. The third is that of a typical British 'work-boat' of the pilot cutter type, slightly rounder than *America* but still basically triangular but very much a heavy displacement midship section. Then comes the midship section of *Jolie Brise*, still full-bodied, but with a slacker bilge and a smoother turn to the garboards. *Dorade* is next and the emergence of a deep fin keel is readily apparent until in the last section, *Myth of Malham*, we have the deep fin keel and the familiar 'champagne glass' section. Notice, incidentally, the length of the underwater periphery of *Myth* compared with, say, *America*, denoting the increase in wetted surface in the lighter yacht.

There are, of course, an infinite number of possible midship sections and now that science is beginning to creep more perceptibly into yacht design I suppose one day someone will classify them, just as aerofoil sections have been numbered. Choosing an appropriate section is one thing. Blending it into the fore and aft lines of the full hull and especially shaping the ends is where the real design skill comes in.

The fore-and-aft shape is determined by the ratio of the maximum beam to the waterline length and, of equal importance, the position of the maximum beam along the length of the hull. This gives us three generic types of yacht hull – where the maximum beam is forward of amidships with the bulk of the hull in the forebody; where the maximum beam is aft of amidships and there is a long lean forebody and a full stern and, finally, the case where the maximum beam is amidships and the displacement distributed evenly fore and aft. In theory, at least, the first of these generic types – known usually as 'cod's head and mackerel tail' – offers the least resistance at speeds where surface friction accounts for the greater proportion of hull drag. It is the least effective however once wave-making begins and at the higher speed/length ratios offers more resistance than the other shapes. In practice, it suffers too from a further disadvantage in that in a seaway it is liable to excessive pitching – a weakness particularly detrimental to getting to windward. As far as their drag characteristics are concerned, there is little to choose between the other two basic fore-and-aft shapes. If anything, the last one – known as the 'wedge' – has a slight advantage over the symmetrical form up to about $V/L^{\frac{1}{2}} = 1.0$ with the latter showing slightly less drag at the higher speeds. These differences are however of importance only when sailing free with the wind generating little in the way of

FIG 5   *Variants of the midship section.*

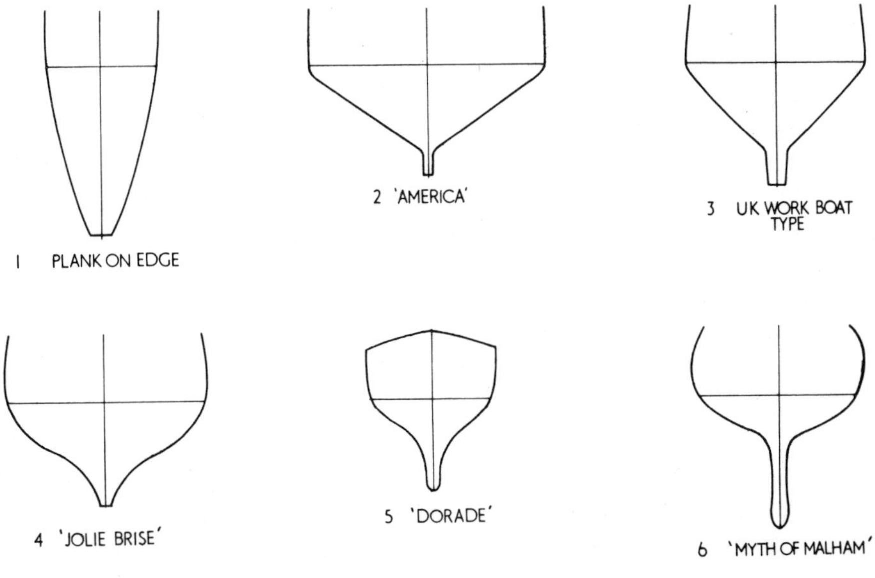

1   PLANK ON EDGE

2   'AMERICA'

3   UK WORK BOAT TYPE

4   'JOLIE BRISE'

5   'DORADE'

6   'MYTH OF MALHAM'

side-force. In providing the lift required to counter side-force the 'canoe body' element of the hull shape itself plays little part and the plan form and hydrofoil section of the keel is all-important. We shall be looking into this in a moment but before leaving the question of fore-and-aft hull shapes we should consider briefly the importance of beam and its relationship to length – the beam/length ratio. In purely theoretical hydrodynamic terms, the optimum beam/length ratio is about 5:1 with the maximum beam about 5 per cent forward of the midships position. At the height of the 'plank-on-edge' period of yacht development many yachts were in fact produced with beam/length ratios of this order. In habitable yachts, however, greater beam is unavoidable and unless excessively high ballast ratios are to be accepted – with all its attendant disadvantages for handling and rating to say nothing of the fact that lead weight is dead weight – adequate beam is an essential concomitant to stability and the ability to carry sail. For these purposes therefore it is usually advantageous to produce a stiffer hull even at the expense of higher resistance. In most modern designs we find that the beam/length ratio is usually of the order of about 2·5:1 to 3:1. The modern tendency too is to position maximum beam aft of the amidships position, sometimes nearly 10 per cent LWL aft but this is determined as much by the need to provide an adequate sheeting base for the large modern overlapping genoas as by hydrodynamic requirements. (We shall be discussing this aspect further in the next chapter.)

In descriptions of the fore-and-aft shapes of hulls in the yachting press one will often see reference to 'wedge' and 'cod's head, mackerel tail' and 'symmetrical' shapes, but also mention is made of either 'block coefficient' or 'prismatic coefficient' in the same context, usually the latter. Block coefficient is the ratio of the immersed volume of the hull (ignoring the fin keel) to that of a block of the same length, breadth and draft. It is not much used for yacht comparisons and the slightly more sophisticated 'prismatic coefficient' (C_p) is used. This is the ratio of the immersed volume of the hull – once again less the fin keel – compared with the volume of a hull where the midship section was constant from end to end of the LWL in the form of a prism. It is therefore a measure of the uniformity along LWL of the immersed volume. In other words, it is determined by the fineness or fullness of the ends in relation to the middle body and the rate at which the beam is faired into the bow and the stern. The greater the C_p the greater the residual resistance of the form of hull. For yachts sailing at displacement speeds, values vary about 0·5 to 0·6 depending upon the sailing conditions for which the hull is designed. Faster sailing craft like catamarans and racing dinghies needing slender hulls with the displacement at the ends as well as amidships usually have a C_p of 0·7 but thereby they sacrifice optimum performance at the lower speeds. Even within the range of cruiser-racer values I have quoted above, the choice of C_p is based on the chosen conditions for optimum performance. The recommended values are:

$V/L^{\frac{1}{2}}$	C_p
less than 1	0·53
1·2	0·58
1·34	0·63
1·5	0·66
1·6	0·68

All this serves to demonstrate the 'horses for courses' aspect of modern yacht design – the need for a higher C if the bulk of the sailing is with the wind aft of the beam compared with that for it on the bow, and whether winds are light or fresh. C_p however is not particuarly critical and since it affects wave-making resistance it is better to have a C_p which is too high rather than one which is too low because at the lower speeds, as we have seen, wave-making accounts for the smaller fraction of total hull drag. But don't expect anybody to tell you what the C_p of a particular yacht is. I have myself never seen it actually quoted except as a relative term used in describing the fullness or otherwise of the underwater ends.

There is also one special shape of yacht which we have not so far considered – the planing hull. Whether it is a single hull or a multi-hulled craft, the ability to plane depends upon three main factors: a low length/weight ratio, that is low displacement for a long waterline length; high power/weight ratio, that is low displacement, large sail area and the stability to carry it; and a hull specifically shaped to generate hydrodynamic lift. In these circumstances, when a hull reaches the upper limits of displacement speed (say $V/L^{\frac{1}{2}} = 1.6$) there is sufficient power from the sails to drive the hull up its own bow wave. The hull is then inclined to the water surface at an optimum angle for the forces of dynamic pressure to begin to have an effect on the specially shaped bottom. The hull begins to emerge slowly from the water, resistance decreases and speed increases. The hull at this stage is then partly supported by her own buoyancy and partly by dynamic lift and this is known as 'semi-planing'. Full planing does not truly begin until the hull is entirely supported by dynamic lift. The semi-planing condition, depending upon the type of boat, occurs between speed/length ratios of about 1·7 to 3·2 and real planing at speeds above that figure.

The characteristic hull shape for planing is that evident in the higher-performance dinghies and in the single hulls of multi-hulled craft – high length/beam ratio, shallow draft and the transition of the waterlines from a V-shaped section at the bow to a flat run aft. Apart from the marvellous variety of offshore catamarans and trimarans which have added a new dimension to ocean-racing and ocean-cruising there have been, from time to time, a number of single-hulled cruiser/racers capable, in the right conditions, of planing, though the majority have not gone beyond the semi-planing stage. One notable exception was a design by the celebrated Dutch designer, E. G. Van de Stadt, called *Black Soo* which achieved the astonishing speed of $V/L^{\frac{1}{2}} = 4.05$ or 22 knots on a LWL of $29\frac{1}{2}$ ft. That she was not outstandingly successful as an ocean-racer merely serves to show again that the right conditions for planing are not found frequently at sea and when they are they are usually of insufficient duration to offset the disadvantages of the planing hull shape in other sailing conditions, particularly getting to windward in a heavy head sea.

Neither semi-planing nor planing should be mistaken for that exhilarating situation which can occur even with the heaviest yacht when the speed of the open sea wave system – and hence its wave length – approaches that of the yacht. Then the yacht gains extra speed when riding down the face of the waves both from the impetus of the surface flow and from the effect of her own weight 'falling downhill'. High speeds can be recorded in these circumstances but they tend to be momentary rather than sustained and have nothing to do with the planing condition.

Let us now look at hull shape from the side – that is, the hull profile or the sheer plan as it is called in line drawings. The line which immediately takes our eye is the sheerline – the line where the deck joins the topsides. This line determines the shape of the hull above the waterline and in particular the all-important element of freeboard. If we look back to the hull shapes in Fig 1, we see at once that the older yachts had much less freeboard than those of today. At the end of the workboat era, the usual proportion of minimum freeboard to waterline length was about 6 or 7 per cent. Nowadays we would expect to see not less than 10 per cent. The shape of the sheerline too will vary considerably from being a straight line to either a 'sprung' curve with the minimum freeboard amidships or reverse sheer where the maximum freeboard is amidships. Given adequate minimum freeboard there is no particular advantage in performance terms to any particular shape or for that matter in rating terms, and one finds all types among the latest designs. Indeed as doghouses and coach roofs begin to disappear in the interest of clear flush decks, the deck line is becoming as important as the sheerline. But what is important is the requirement for adequate freeboard. Freeboard gives a greater range of stability, it reduces resistance when heeled because the lee-rail is kept clear of the water, decks are drier and, overall, safer places to work on in a seaway. Freeboard too gives extra reserve buoyancy and buoyancy too which can be used in the extra accommodation it also makes available. Its main drawback may be that it tends to increase windage and to raise the centre of gravity of the hull. Anyone however who has sailed in one of those Edwardian inshore half-tide rocks in a Channel chop will be in no doubt that adequate freeboard is the supreme boon and blessing of modern design. Its contribution to seaworthiness is well recognised by the rating advantages it continues to be afforded.

Below the waterline the sheer plan shows us the shape of keel, the rudder and the profile of the ends or overhangs. Also, the amount of actual hull – excluding keel and appendages – below the waterline is an indication of displacement and how it is distributed. The depth of the canoe body from waterline to the bilge taken at various points and averaged out – mean depth immersed (MDI) – when taken together with LWL and beam gives a close approximation of a yacht's displacement. It is employed in rating rules in preference to displacement itself because of the practical difficulties of measuring the latter value accurately (see chapter 5). Depth too, as indicated by the sheer plan, can give us some indication of the wave-making propensities of the hull shape. A hull which is too deep amidships for its length – a situation usually met in the heavier displacement designs – tends to produce a heavy quarter wave which may need vastly more energy to sustain it than would a shallow wave. The energy needed to produce a wave varies approximately as the square of its depth – a 2 ft wave requiring four times the energy of a 1 ft wave. In shaping a hull therefore the object is to produce not just a long wave system but also a shallow one. As we have seen, waterline length or effective sailing length determines the former. The depth of the hull and its displacement determines the latter.

To mitigate this problem of the massive quarter waves produced by some hulls when travelling at high speed, modern design has produced the 'bustle'. The dictionary definition of bustle is 'a pad or frame added to the buttocks to flare out a woman's skirt behind' and our Victorian forbears no doubt thought them fast when they were first introduced. Our yachting 'bustle' is also a filling out of the buttocks of the after body of a yacht – there is a rather exaggerated example on Fig 6 – and the intention here is to make the water flow over the hull and under it behave as if the yacht were slightly longer than it is. It is a process that requires careful design to ensure that the gain in reduced wave-making resistance at the higher speeds is not offset by an increase in frictional drag at lower speeds. Tank tests have shown that the bustle works best at speeds of $V/L^{\frac{1}{2}} = 1\cdot2$ and above where total drag may be reduced by as much as 8 per cent. This could correspond to a speed increase of between 1 and 2 per cent – a race-winning margin for most events. Our bustle then, too, is fast.

Although there is no evidence that the Victorians tried bustles on their yachts as well as on their women they were well aware of the speed-producing aspects of long overhangs fore and aft. There was also the added advantage that long overhangs assisted in keeping the rig

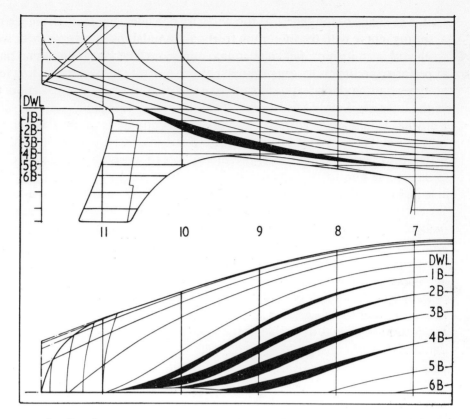

FIG 6   *Bustle.*

all inboard and either removed the need for bowsprits and bumpkins or allowed them to be reduced. Further, the heavy displacement of these earlier yachts gave them a tendency to plunge in a seaway and they greatly benefited from the addition of buoyant bows and sterns. The large inshore classes for a long time made a fetish of long ends and the great pre-war 'J' class yachts had overhangs of as much as 50 per cent of the LWL. Even today, those most elegant of inshore racers, the 12 m yachts which contend from time to time for the America's Cup, boast up to 60 per cent LWL in overhangs. Modern cruiser-racers are in general 'short-ended'. With light to moderate displacement being the normal vogue, short overhangs appear adequate to maintain reserve buoyancy which acts to damp pitching. Long, full ends tend to cause slamming when sailing to windward. Nor is any extra weight desirable at the extremities of the hull, and with modern high aspect ratio rigs there is little difficulty in keeping the sail plan inboard. Bows therefore tend to vary little and although sterns still come in a number of varieties they are usually variations of the 'chopped off' counter called for by the modern tendency to mount a separate skeg and rudder – the main variation being in the position of the chop.

As a glance back to Fig 1 will show, the most obvious change in the profile of the offshore cruiser-racer has been in that of the fin keel. It is here too that scientific investigation and tank testing have made their greatest impact upon hull design. The fin contributes by far the greater proportion of the side force for least drag of the body/keel combination – something like 80 per cent of the lift for 50 per cent of the drag. From our discussion earlier in the chapter on the elements of the sailing mechanism, the function of the fin keel is to generate lift to counter the side-force imposed by the wind upon the yacht's sails and to generate as much water lift as possible in conjunction with the least drag – in other words to have a high lift/drag ratio. Further, since leeway angle and heel cannot be eliminated, the fin must operate to its best effect at varying angles of incidence to the water-flow. Experiments over many years have produced as close to a finite answer as is possible in a situation with so many variables and the result is shown in *Noreyma*'s profile in Fig 1. The ideal section is that which we considered before when discussing the fore-and-aft shape of the hull – about a 20 per cent thickness to chord ratio with a parabolic nose – that is rounded rather than sharpened so as not to reduce the safe range of angles of incidence – and the maximum thickness at about 45 per cent of the chord. There is also a slight advantage in having the trailing edge blunted rather than tapered off. In plan form, a slightly trailing fin of almost square proportions and a highish aspect ratio (say keel depth^2/keel area $= 2$) seems to provide a compromise of low drag, good manoeuvrability and constancy of centre of lateral resistance leading to directional stability. For most normal yacht speeds, the fin position is somewhat forward of the underwater midships position. The optimum angle – sweepback – of the leading edge of the fin keel is about 40°–45°.

One other very apparent difference in the keel profiles of recent yachts compared with those of even a decade or so ago is the separation of the rudder from the keel and its installation on a separate skeg placed well aft. This again is sensible, and scientific evolution has not been impeded by rating considerations. The efficiency of modern sail plans and the high/lift drag ratio of a well-designed fin keel due to its efficient aspect ratio and effective longitudinal cross section permit its area to be considerably reduced and placed, as we have seen, at the optimum position on the canoe body – about amidships. This midships position coupled with the need to rake the fin trailing edge aft to reduce wetted surfaces makes it an unsatisfactory place to hang the rudder both from the hydrodynamic and the engineering point of view. In the early 1960s many light displacement yachts still retained their rudders in the traditional position, and, as the late Sir Francis Chichester discovered to his cost in *Gipsy Moth IV*, whilst their ability to windward was unsurpassed they tended to become uncontrollable at high speeds when running and reaching. The device of dropping a removable skeg through the cockpit sole was only a partial remedy. The solution came first with the introduction of the spade rudder – that is a rudder hung clear of the fin – and finally the skeg and rudder. The main advantage of the skeg is that it increases the efficiency of a given area of rudder and increases the angle at which stalling is likely to occur. It also allows a rudder of smaller area and higher aspect ratio to be fitted and this serves to reduce tiller loads.

In considering the effects of beam upon general hull performance we touched briefly upon its function in giving us a stiffer hull – that is its contribution to the major task of the hull in carrying sail. The main factor here is the righting stability of the hull which is, as we have seen, intimately connected with such factors as seakindliness, dryness, directional stability and, ultimately, with safety. Stability depends upon having a low centre of gravity for the hull and this can be achieved by hanging the ballast low, and also by a hull shape that ensures that the centre of buoyancy of the hull swings well off to leeward when the yacht heels and this, as we have seen, is encouraged by big beam and high freeboard. In broad terms narrow, heavily ballasted boats are tender initially but stiffen up rapidly as the angle of heel increases. Beamy boats on the other hand have greater initial stiffness but tend to heel further once the weather bilge is out of the water. These factors face the designer with the

Right: *view of* America *from the port quarter.*

Left: *a Falmouth quay-punt of the type which was the model of the British offshore yacht until the mid-fifties. This is an early example, but note the long straight keel and the full bow. Offshore racing skippers will also note the open-handed self-denial of the gaffer in offering first choice of food to his crew.* Plus ça change!

Top: Henrietta, Vesta *and* Fleetwing *off Sandy Hook at the start of the Great Atlantic Race of 1866. The race started on 11 December and the first two yachts finished on Christmas Day! On 19 December, whilst hove-to in a gale,* Fleetwing *lost six men – four seamen and two quartermasters – overboard. Despite the hours spent searching for them she still made 199 miles during that day – and finished only eight hours behind the winner,* Henrietta. *The prize was $90,000.*
Bottom: *the English schooner* Cambria *and the American schooner* Dauntless *at the start of their uphill transatlantic race from Daunt Rock, Ireland to Sandy Hook, New York. The start was in July 1870 – summer instead of winter as in 1866, and old salts were heard to mutter that the offshore breed was getting soft.* Cambria *won by the remarkable margin of only 1 hour 43 minutes.*

subtle problem of deciding the proportion of form (i.e. beam) stability to weight stability to choose. Once again, the designer's choice will be influenced by the optimum conditions for which he is designing his yacht. Hull drag due to heel is not significant up to about 20° but thereafter from 30° onwards – especially if the lee rail is immersed – drag very rapidly increases. Large angles of heel too are undesirable in that they involve a loss of both sail efficiency and side-force generation plus, of course, increased leeway angle. Hanging ballast low, however, can have penalties in both increased wetted surface – remember that fin areas add appreciably to wetted surface – and hence light-airs performance and, as we shall see, some rating penalty is also possible. Displacement for a given waterline length will also be increased and this in its turn may mean deeper wave systems with effects upon performance off the wind in strong winds. Furthermore, very stiff boats impose greater strains on their masts and rigging. On the other hand, in light or medium displacement yachts considerable beam need not add unduly to resistance as beam on such yachts tends to narrow appreciably as the yacht heels. Modern design experience, analysis of the performance of full-scale yachts and test-tank models has, as we saw earlier, settled on a range of beam length ratios of about 2·5 to 3:1 and ballast ratios – the weight of the ballast keel expressed as a percentage of the displacement of the yacht – of between 40 and 50 per cent, depending upon the type of yacht. This latter figure is, of course, always somewhat suspect because the addition of crew, stores and equipment may well vary a yacht's displacement significantly upwards and make nonsense of the designed ballast-ratio figure. It is for this reason that one hears a good deal less chat about ballast ratio than used to be the case – coupled with the fact that modern GRP and alloy construction methods make for stronger, lighter hulls. Once again, however, there are no set rules about form stability and weight stability and it does not necessarily follow that a large beam ratio means a low ballast ratio or the reverse. The following figures which are for a range of yachts designed by a number of well-known American designers to meet the requirement of the One Ton Cup – that is a rating of 27·5 ft under the IOR Mark III rule – illustrate what I mean:

Beam/length ratio	Ballast ratio (%)
2·4	48
2·4	48
2·7	44
2·5	33
2·5	48
3·1	53
2·4	40

– and these figures are for yachts intended to compete against each other on level terms!

Whereas the table above illustrates a point I have made frequently in this chapter and will do again throughout the book – that within optimum design criteria arrived at by scientific analysis there is still room for infinite variety – nonetheless, there are a number of arithmetical factors which are invaluable in comparing one yacht with another on the basis of potential performance. Putting this another way, we can quantify into a usable arithmetical shorthand for comparison purposes many of the hull factors we have discussed throughout this chapter.

You will recall that displacement (W) decreases speed because of the volume of water being pushed aside but waterline length (LWL) increases speed because greater length produces longer and hence faster waves. We can therefore relate the two values in the factor $W/(L/100)^3$ which indicates the density of the displacement. The displacement W is given in tons and L (LWL) in feet (a linear measure), and as displacement is a measure of volume we make the two values mathematically compatible by cubing the waterline length. You will quite frequently come across this factor in books and articles on design where it is called the 'displacement-length' ratio. Its significance – as no doubt you will have realised – is that the lower the value of the displacement-length ratio, the greater will be the speed of the yacht provided that it is capable of carrying the appropriate area of sail. Displacement-length ratios of less than 250 indicate 'light displacement' among cruiser-racers and anything over about 350 'heavy displacement'. One other value of interest is that 150 is about the upper limit for any boat to be able to plane.

As we were reminded earlier in the chapter, the basic efficiency of any vehicle is largely determined by its power/weight ratio, which in the case of sailing machines is sail area to displacement. Sometimes this ratio is used directly – so many square feet of sail to each ton of displacement. On this basis the average cruiser racer carries between 100 and 150 ft²/ton and lighter craft (like say the *Flying Dutchman*) carry the equivalent of around 600 ft²/ton. In round figures, something like 400 ft² of sail per ton of displacement is needed to provide the power to reach planing conditions. In order, however, to allow for the scaling factor when comparing boats of marked difference in size, the more usual practice is to use the ratio of Sail area/$W^{\frac{2}{3}}$. Here the *Flying Dutchman* would have 345 ft²/ton, the average cruiser-racer around 150, and planing craft would require a minimum of 280.

Looking at these two major ratios in conjunction, we would expect to achieve optimum sail performance off the wind when $W/(L/100)^3$ is small and $SA/W^{\frac{2}{3}}$ is large. However, as we have seen, the power to carry the optimum amount of sail does not depend upon the displacement but upon the stability of the hull. It is therefore useful to compare the product of the length/beam ratio and the $SA/W^{\frac{2}{3}}$ ratio to allow for stability which, if we assume for the moment that all yachts have a sail plan of ideal aspect-ratio, is a measure of the sail heeling moment divided by the hull righting moment. The ballast ratio is also an indication of stability and the power to carry sail.

In chapter 1 we saw that over the century or so of yacht development since *America* launched the modern era of yachting, the most marked improvements have occurred in best speed made good to windward (V_{mg}). When comparing hull factors which contribute to such improvements, therefore, we need to look at three other ratios: the length/draught ratio: the aspect ratio of the fin keel; and the ratio of sail area to wetted surface. This latter, of course, is useful for all points of sailing which, like sailing to windward, occur below $V/L^{\frac{1}{2}} = 1$ when skin-friction accounts for the major proportion of hull drag. It is however a difficult value to quantify unless one has access to design data and drawings.

We now have a considerable number of factors and ratios by which we can compare one yacht with another. To give a broad idea of general trends in published designs over the last century or so I have tabulated the main characteristics of outstanding yachts for each period in Appendix A. We shall be looking at these trends with particular interest in the last chapter on the shape of yachts to come but I would end this one with the caveat that though there are many ways of comparing one yacht with another it is winning races which is the final test and here rating is the comparator which counts.

3

The Way of a Yacht in the Wind

When we revised our knowledge of the basic sailing diagram at the beginning of the last chapter, we saw from Fig 4 that the optimum sailing angle (i.e. the best course to windward) was determined by the sum of the two drag angles – the drag angle for the hull and that for the sails. These angles are themselves determined by the respective lift/drag ratios of the hull and the sails and to achieve the best performance to windward these two angles have to be kept to a minimum. In other words, we need the maximum lift/drag ratio from the sails and from the hull. But which, one might ask, is the more important?

Put in general terms: can more be accomplished in improving sailing-craft performance by concentrating on sails rather than on hulls? This is a favourite topic for discussion among yachtsmen everywhere. It has the supreme merit of all such enduring topics – like which is the better end to open an egg – of having no definitive answer. Some yachtsmen believe that because a sail can be seen to be setting well and sail efficiency can be adjusted in response to visual judgement, sails are more important. Others, that because the drag on a hull can almost be felt physically by those on board, hull efficiency matters most. Both views of course are equally right and the answer is that both factors are of equal importance. Let us however look a little deeper.

For purposes of comparison and analysis it is convenient to separate hull and sails as I have done in this book. For scientific examination we put the sails in the wind tunnel and the yacht hull in the testing tank. In all but a very few limited circumstances, however, we can only test sails and hulls together in a real yacht sailing in the real wind on the real sea. We could for example produce an aerofoil (a glider wing, for example) which would have a drag angle as low as 3° and a hydrofoil hull with one of 5° so that, in theory, the whole assembly should be able to sail at 8° to the apparent wind. (This would also incidentally occur at a speed around three times that of the wind!) In practice, the best that has so far been achieved, even in perfect conditions by specially designed and rigged craft, is no better than about 20° to the apparent wind. When we come to even the most weatherly of displacement yachts, again under ideal conditions, 27° to the apparent wind at a speed to windward (V_{mg}) of about two-thirds the true wind-speed is about the best we can expect. At 27° to the apparent wind, sail drag (aerodynamic drag angle ε) probably accounts for about 10° and hull drag (hydrodynamic drag angle δ) for 17°, which could suggest that there is in fact more room for improvement in the hull than the sails. It may be that hull drag could be reduced but if we assume that in achieving 27° off the apparent wind both sails and hull are working at maximum efficiency an improvement to hull performance might mean that whilst the hull was capable of going faster or closer to the wind, the sails at the extra speed and closer angle of incidence were no longer operating at their best efficiency because of sheeting angle limitations or because extra heel reduces the driving power (lift/drag ratio) of the sail plan. We must not forget that both sail plan and hull must always be capable of adequate performance at all points of sailing. The main point here is of course that hull and sail factors are inseparable and of equal importance and the adjustment of one will require an adjustment of the other to balance it and we can never be sure that by improving the one we are necessarily improving the other.

We are dealing here with yachts already performing at or close to their optimum and of advancing the whole state of the art. I am not suggesting that a good hull with poor sails will not improve its windward performance by having a new set of properly cut sails or even a new sail plan, or that a new keel and rudder might not do wonders for a yacht with a reasonable set of sails. There are plenty of excellent examples of both in the racing circuits and the archtype in the Solent is undoubtedly that grand old yacht *Cynthia* which, with a modern set of sails on a hull designed and built in 1910, certainly as recently as the mid-1960s frightened the pants off modern racing craft nearly sixty years her junior. What we are considering is a situation where we are, if you like, trying to push forward the frontiers of performance into new territory. An analogy here might be that of cars and aeroplanes – what sort of result would we have achieved with, say, a Jaguar XJ 12 power unit in a Model T Ford chassis or jet engines in an Anson or a 'Goony Bird' (DC 3) fuselage? And who is to say which matters most – the propulsion or the propelled?

Having looked briefly at the sails and hull in combination again, let us now remove the hull and take a closer look at the mast and sails. It is common practice to compare the action of sails in the wind with that of wings in flight and there is little doubt that the evolution of efficient sail plans owes a great deal to the ever-growing store of knowledge accumulating from aeronautical practice. Wings, however, are devices for generating lift and except in certain special situations the inevitable resultant drag is merely an unavoidable concomitant to the lift-generating process. With sails, however, whilst we require good lift characteristics for sailing to windward, once we are off the wind our main interest is in the drag characteristics of the sail. Another way of putting this is that sails operate up to angles of incidence of 90° whereas aircraft wings rarely exceed 20°. The elasticity of the material of which sails are made means too that they change shape with the wind force acting upon them and hence it is far more difficult to derive their aerodynamic characteristics by theory and calculation than it is for a fixed wing section. Also, wings operate at higher airspeeds and they operate too without the complications – at least nowadays – imposed by spars and rigging. We cannot therefore simply accept unqualified all aerodynamic theory stemming from aeroplane experience, but until places like Southampton University, the Stevens Institute of Technology in the United States, and other institutions where they think about sailing problems have produced a comparative body of knowledge, we have no other guide.

Let us begin first by looking at basic aerodynamic sections. If we incline a flat plate to the wind we get lift at right angles to the windstream and drag in the direction of the stream (see Fig 7). The amount of lift and drag we get will vary with the angle of the plate to the stream and we shall examine the effects of changing this angle – the angle of incidence as it is called – later on. Very roughly, at about 20° incidence angle, the flat plate will give us a lift/drag ratio of 1:1. If we give the plate a slight curve downwind – that is, like the camber of a sail – we improve the lift/drag ratio to about 7:1. If we go further and give the plate thickness as well as camber and streamline the shape, we can raise the lift/drag ratio to the order of 20:1. We are, however, now departing from the more usual profile of sails and I include this last example to indicate what is attainable in theory in the way of lift/drag ratios by comparatively simple procedures. (We shall be exploring the potentialities of giving thickness to sails in the last chapter of the book.)

48

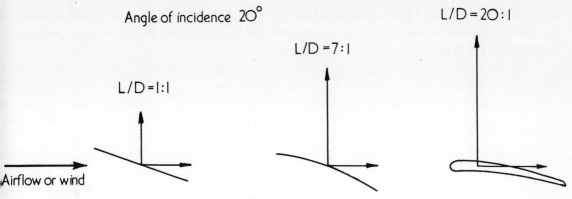

Angle of incidence 20°

L/D=1:1

L/D =7:1

L/D = 20:1

Airflow or wind

FIG 7   *The relationship between lift and drag.*

The reason we get more lift from both the cambered plate and the aerofoil section results from pressure distribution over its surfaces. Pressure comes from two sources: increased pressure to the windward side of the plate and reduced pressure on the leeward side. The increased pressure comes from the impact of the wind and the reduced pressure from the increased velocity of the wind as it flows over the lee-surface and 'sucks' at the sail just as the wind sometimes sucks the roof of a fabric car hood. The actual pressures over the lee-side of the sail are shown in Fig 8.

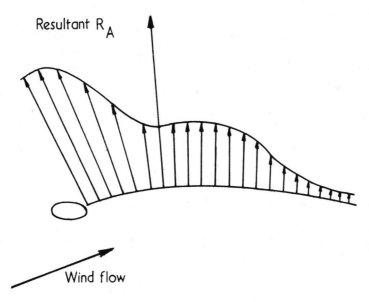

Resultant R_A

Wind flow

FIG 8   *Pressures on the lee-side of a mainsail.*

The example I have chosen here is that of a Bermudian mainsail attached to a mast. The kink in the pressure distribution is caused by the disturbance to the flow by the mast and serves to demonstrate why sails are not directly comparable with wings and, incidentally, why staysails have a better set than mainsails and area for area are more effective. Since we are talking about wind pressure, notice that maximum pressure is along the line of the luff and hence why a gap between mast and sail loses valuable drive through leaks. Let us also look at pressure distribution over the sail surface in plan. The pressure values are shown in

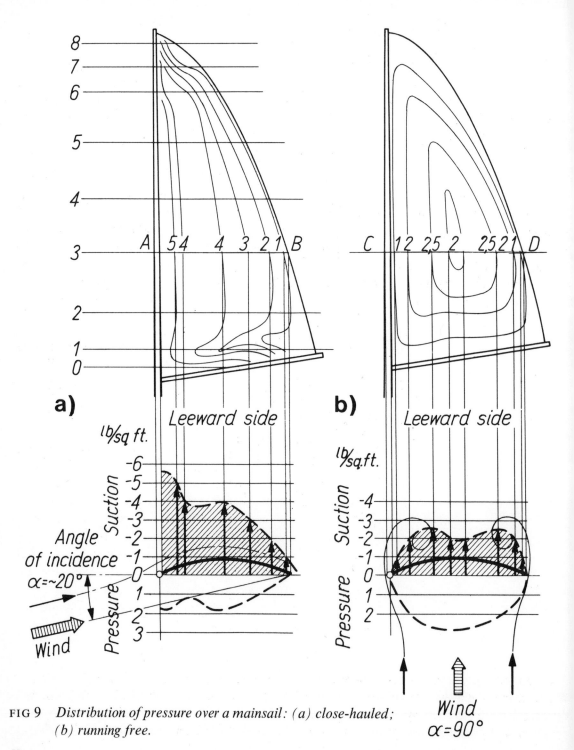

FIG 9   *Distribution of pressure over a mainsail: (a) close-hauled;*
       (b) running free.

the form of contours or, if you like, isobars like those on weather charts. The first is for a mainsail close-hauled, i.e. maximum lift/drag ratio – wind angle about 20° – the second is with the sail set for running, i.e. maximum drag – wind angle about 90°. Notice that with the close-hauled sail the pressure is distributed fairly evenly about the middle of the sail but is uneven along the boom and at the peak and notice, too, how the high pressure along the luff falls rapidly in the mast wind-shadow. The turbulence along the boom and at the head of the sail is caused by air 'leaking' over the edge of the sail from windward to leeward because of the different pressures. (It occurs, in fact, all round the sail.) The turbulence is known as 'end effect' and occurs in all aerofoils – and hydrofoils like fin keels for that matter – and its adverse effects can to some extent be reduced by making the luff of the sail as long as possible – that is increasing the aspect ratio – and by adopting an elliptical shape to the head by an adequate roach. (The Spitfire wing shape is the classic elliptical aerofoil.) At the boom end large flat booms offer some advantage aerodynamically but many disadvantages in other respects.

Pressure distribution is, as will be seen, completely different for the downwind sail. Here the pressures are lower because the air attempts to flow round the mast and the leach and is 'separated' – it breaks away in large eddies – and the pressure differential between the windward and the leeward side is much reduced. Also, in the downwind case the apparent wind is reduced in velocity by the forward speed of the yacht whereas of course when sailing to windward it is increased.

From these examples it is apparent that the pressures generated by a sail and hence the driving force will depend upon two major factors – the angle of incidence and the camber of the sail. When we talk about angle of incidence of sails we usually mean the angle of the yacht sail to the apparent wind – the wind-course angle. This assumes that the sail is properly trimmed for that particular wind-course angle because, of course, angle of incidence is under the control of the crew: on the wind with the rudder; off the wind with the sheet. We also disregard the complications of heel for the time being. As we have seen, the lift/drag ratio is determined by the camber of the sail and its angle of incidence. If we alter the angle of incidence to obtain more lift, we inevitably also get more drag. For any particular sail, however, lift and drag do not change at the same rate for a change in angle of incidence and the relationship between these three values is shown graphically at Fig 10. As we might expect, the maximum lift/drag ratios occur close to the wind – the smaller the sail drag angle the closer we can sail, hull factors permitting – whereas there is no lift at all when running. Other points to notice are that this particular diagram would apply in reality only to a particular sail of given plan form, cut, camber and area, made of a particular type of material in weight, porosity and surface finish. It is also only applicable to a particular wind-speed. If any of these variables is changed then the shape of the diagram would also vary. Again, the diagram would apply only to a single sail and disregards the effects of other sails in the whole sailplan and also those of masts and spars. In short it is an idealised picture of what a sail can produce in theory – the type of data displayed here is obtainable only as the result of wind-tunnel tests – and once again a sail without a hull and the effects that a hull would have. Nonetheless it is a useful as a basis for understanding what the main factors are in the efficiency of any sail plan.

Let us look first at the question of planform – bermuda, gaff and square. The key to efficiency is once again that of aspect ratio as it was in the case of keel profiles. We use the same basis – span²/total area – and in this case, span means the length of the luff. The type of Bermudian sail which modern masting permits will have an aspect ratio (AR) of 6 and we shall find mainsails and foresails of this AR on most modern offshore racers. Earlier Bermudian sails and those of pure cruising yachts will have a lower aspect ratio of about 3; gaff mainsails come out at AR = 1 and for square rig, about $\frac{1}{3}$. At Fig 11 I have drawn diagrams of the characteristics of each of these sails of the same area but different planform to give an indication of their lift/drag ratios for various angles of incidence. It demonstrates clearly the importance of high AR sails for sailing close-hauled. The optimum value is probably that of a luff/foot ratio of about 3 of a well-roached sail. Increasing the AR in practice does not bring continuous improvements to windward ability largely on account of the tendency for very narrow mainsails to be subject to twist and for the area of effective lift to be reduced by the high relative size of the mast. Other factors also limit height of rig – increased heeling moment, and the problems of weight aloft.

The best reaching sails are those with an AR of about 1. Here the gaff rig comes into its

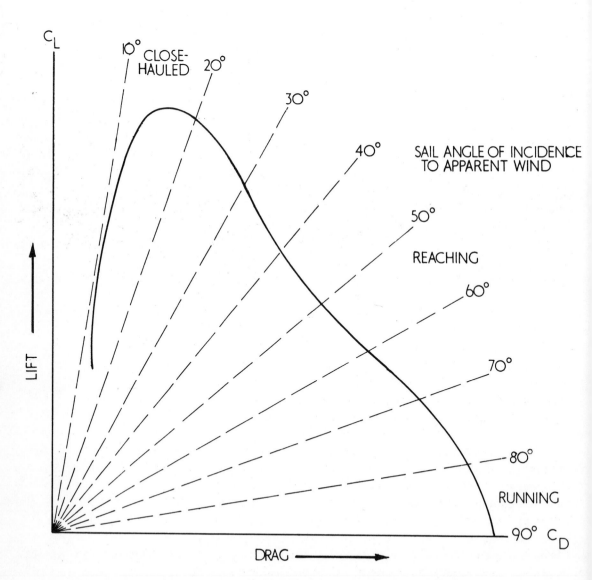

FIG 10 *The lift and drag characteristics of a sail at varying angles of incidence.*

Above: *the great classic* Cambria *lithographic 'shot' which looks down on the dining room of the* RORC *(and no doubt many other yacht clubs). It serves to remind us all that there once was a time when yachts challenging for the America's Cup had to sail the Atlantic first – to the greater benefit of yachting as a whole. A few days after finishing her race across the Atlantic,* Cambria *was beaten in her attempt to regain the America's Cup.*

Over page
Page 54: Jolie Brise, *winner of the first Fastnet. Although of French origin – she was a Le Havre pilot boat – she typifies the British offshore yacht of the first half of the twentieth century. Her owner – the immortal Lt-Com E. G. Martin – once said of her breed: '. . . it seems to me to be far more important that (she) should be steady and comfortable in rough water than that she should sail very fast.'*

Page 55: Dorade, *designed and owned by Olin Stephens, won the Fastnet in 1931 and 1933 by a large margin. She brought two new classic names to the sport – the dorade vent (quite clearly visible in this photograph) – and that of her designer.*

Myth of Malham – *the greatest. Her remarkable career came to a fitting end in 1972 when she was quietly sunk off the Brittany coast.*

own and this was the rig of the famous schooners we discussed in chapter 1 – *America* was clearly at her best point of sailing when reaching, though her performance to windward compared with her contemporaries was also superior because of her flatter, closer-woven sails. Square rig, as we might expect, gives its best performance when running and is not really effective at all at angles of incidence closer than 45° to the apparent wind.

Square sails are not things often seen nowadays outside the confines of the Tall Ships Race but for cruising long distances downwind – through the Trade Winds for example – they are invaluable unless one has a crew large enough to keep a tame spinnaker. One of the best-known examples seen in UK waters every other year or so is that of Group-Captain Carr's well-known *Havfruen III* sister ship to Nansen's famed *Fram*, designed in 1897 by the Norwegian Colin Archer. *Havfruen III* spends a great deal of her time in the West Indies and on Transatlantic passages and she boasts an even more unusual sail than a squaresail in the shape, literally, of a 'raffee'.

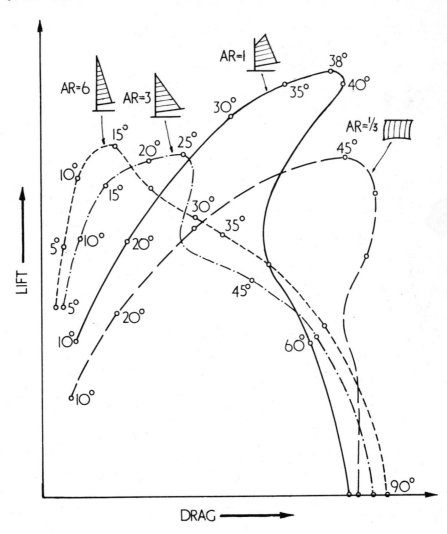

FIG 11 *Comparison of lift-drag curves for sails of differing aspect ratios based on model tests.*

Whatever planform a sail may have, however, it will not work efficiently unless it has adequate camber. As we saw earlier there is a massive improvement in lift/drag ratio when a flat plate is given a slight camber. The optimum value for camber depends upon wind strength and, inevitably, on the type of hull we are seeking to drive. (There is simply no escape from the interplay of hull and sail factors!) For cruiser/racers the value of depth of the camber – the bow of the sail – to its width (chord) is about 1/10. For heavier, less easily driven hulls, probably about 1/7. It is worth noting here that when close-hauled, full-cut, deep-cambered sails give significantly more heeling moment than flatter sails and here too, the hull factors can impose a limit. On most modern mainsails we have some control of the degree of camber by means of either a zip fastener along the foot or a line pulled through the 'Cunningham' hole. But the position of the maximum camber also matters. For beating about halfway along the chord of the sail; for reaching about 60 per cent are the optimum theoretical values. In practice, the relationship between the flow under the headsail and across the main plays an important part and the most practical position for maximum camber is about $\frac{1}{3}$ along the chord. We can also adjust this point too by the leech line. As far as camber is concerned, however, the importance of the amount of camber a sail has exceeds that where the maximum position occurs.

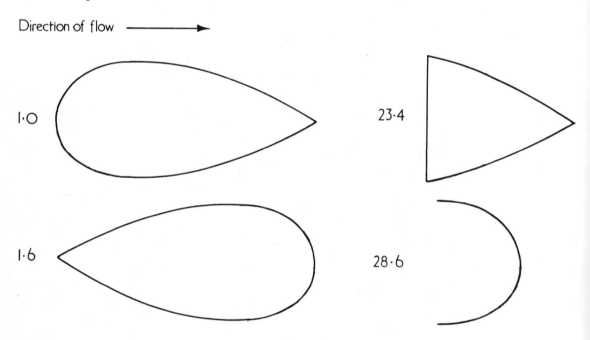

FIG 12   *Drag forces acting on shapes of the same cross-sectional area.*

Camber too is of great importance in sails used off the wind. Here, as we have seen, we are interested in achieving maximum drag. If we look therefore at a few fundamental shapes of the same cross-sectional area in an airstream (Fig 12) our 'cod's head and mackerel tail' from the last chapter has a relative drag force of 1·0. If we turn it round and make a 'wedge', the drag increases to 1·6. If we turn it back and flatten off the leading edge to make a flat plate, the drag rises to 23·4. Finally if we offer the open face of a hemisphere to the wind we get a relative drag force of 28·6. You don't have to be a sailor moreover to appreciate the practical

58

effects of these figures: just try gybing an open umbrella on a windy day. Which, of course, brings us to spinnakers.

The spinnaker is a truly modern sail and most of its development has taken place within the memory of many yachtsmen sailing today. A well-known anthology on cruising and ocean-racing written in the mid-1920s describes the spinnaker as 'a light weather triangular sail boomed out from the mast on the opposite side to a (gaff) mainsail'. (The origin of the word, incidentally, is believed to come from the name *Sphinx* – that of the Edwardian yacht which first flew one. Curiously enough, it owes nothing to the earlier sail called a 'spanker' which was a small gaff mizzen on a full-rigged ship.) The writer then goes on to say:

> Quite frankly I prefer to see the spinnaker confined to racing craft and its place taken in a purely cruising yacht by an efficient squaresail . . . but for ordinary estuary cruising and for summer coastal work, no doubt the spinnaker will hold its own for some time to come.

How right he was!

Originally regarded merely as a bag to catch the wind when running, the spinnaker is now probably the most important sail in the inventory, with an area usually well in excess of that of the main and the largest genoa. Indeed, it now tends to replace the latter as a headsail on all points of sailing from the dead-run to a close reach. There are as far as I can discover no statistics to show how much more frequently the spinnaker is flown now than say in the late 1950s when ocean-racing as a sport began to take-off. Two things have certainly happened. First, spinnakers are now carried in wind-strengths which would have been unthinkable twenty years ago and they are also carried increasingly close to the wind. For both these developments, though much is due to better gear and rigging and general handling technique, the main credit should go to the sailmakers for evolving better methods of cutting sails and to the fabric makers for superior sailcloths.

Naturally, these developments in cut and cloth are not confined only to spinnakers. All sails have been improved as a result of them. It is however in the spinnaker, which is essentially a light responsive sail, that their results are most apparent. All sails perform best if they keep their shape (camber) and don't develop creases and folds or suffer from bulky seams. When these defects develop in mainsails and the heavier headsails it may be some time before they become noticeable. A creased or misshapen spinnaker is as obvious as an unpressed morning suit at a society wedding.

Because of the strains to which they are subjected, all sails tend to stretch out of shape and one of the main qualities of the modern synthetic materials like Dacron and Terylene is that they have a high resistance to stretch and tend to recover their shape rapidly after strain. This is largely due to the inherent elasticity of the component fibres and also to the tightness of the weave and the technique of heat crimping so that the fibres have a 'memory' as it were of their original position. This same technique will also give our wedding guest a permanent crease in his trousers. 'Permanent' in the case of sails tends, with the very great strains often involved in racing, to be a short-lived condition and other means have to be found in order to minimise distortion. Various techniques are employed to establish the directions of the main tensions of a sail under load and the knowledge is employed in giving maximum resistance to distortion by panelling, cutting and sewing the sailcloth. Spinnakers have shown the greatest sea-change here both in the width of their panels and in the direction of their seams or cut. Starting with the style used in the late 1950s with vertical seams between the panels, spinnakers have progressed through diagonal cut – the Herbulot type – through horizontal cut – made necessary by the increasing requirement to carry the spinnaker on ever close reaches – finally to today's 'star-cut' reaching spinnakers.

But in addition to their resistance to distortion, modern sail materials have also advantages in that their very tight weave reduces porosity and hence leaks between the high and low pressure surfaces of the sail and also in their surface smoothness. Just as we seek 'laminar-flow' over the hull surfaces to obtain a better lift/drag ratio by drastically reducing the drag, so too we seek laminar-flow over the sail surfaces where this is possible. Once again, however, small boats – of dinghy size – are more likely to achieve laminar flow over parts of their sails than are larger craft hence the tendency to 'dress' dinghy sails.

So far we have considered sails in isolation – sails like mainsails and genoas producing maximum lift when close-hauled and spinnakers producing maximum drag when running. We now have to consider the effects of multiple sails and the interaction of mainsails and headsails.

In general terms, the efficiency of a well-designed sail depends in practice on the means by which it is attached to the hull. As we saw from Fig 11, there is a considerable disturbance to the flow over a mainsail caused by the mast. Masted sails for this reason do not perform as well in terms of drive force per square foot as do sails attached to stays. In other words, headsails and staysails are more efficient than mainsails and mizzen on all points of sailing other than, possibly, a really hard beat. This fact, among others, explains why the size of headsails has steadily increased over the years and that it is now customary for the size of the fore-triangle to exceed that of the mainsail and for the largest genoa to exceed the size of the main by as much as 80 per cent. The efficiency of the sails which are set flying – like spinnakers, spinnaker staysails, and tall boys and a very flat cut spinnaker (rather erroneously called the 'spanker') – is an area of intense and interesting development. As we have already discussed, off the wind much depends upon shape, cut and weight of material. But as we have seen, the modern tendency is to carry spinnakers and similar sails closer and closer to the wind. Here the main problem is keeping the luff taut and preventing it from curling over, creating turbulent flow over the lee – lifting – surface of the sail. The star-cut is one method of meeting this problem and no doubt others will emerge despite the fairly severe restriction placed upon spinnakers in the International Offshore Rule like the prohibiting of battens and the penalising of headboards.

From the point of view of actual sail efficiency, therefore, the ideal sail plan might be one of staysails alone with spinnakers for downwind work; next would come the foresail plus masted mainsail with spinnakers and, finally, the single-masted mainsail without headsails – the Finn rig. There have of course been yachts which have sailed satisfactorily with each of these various combinations. In the 1972 *Observer* Single Handed Transatlantic Race, *Vendredi Treize*, the Carter-designed runner-up, had three boomed staysails making up her 'schooner' rig. She was however deliberately under-canvassed and the objective here was to avoid her solitary helmsman from exhausting himself by too frequent sail changes. The redoubtable Finn class dinghy, on the other hand, has a single-masted mainsail. In her case, however, the disadvantages inherent in masted sails are greatly reduced by the unstayed mast being free to rotate in its step under the turning leverage of the main boom which is rigidly attached to it. Such things are possible in 15 ft inshore racing boats, but a great deal more difficult in the bigger 'blue-water' classes. In theory the ideal sail would be something like a kite and from time to time one sees experiments being conducted into such ideas. High theory suggests that such sails, if they could be persuaded to fly at even 80 per cent from directly downwind, could take a yacht to windward. Here again, however, we are dealing with small hull and small sails and theory and practice will have to advance considerably before they can be applied offshore. Modern large-size spinnakers in a strong gusty wind possess enough of the untamed element for most of us.

The traditional foresail-plus-masted-mainsail-plus-spinnaker rig seems likely to prevail in habitable offshore yachts for some time to come despite the willingness of owners and designers and crews to experiment. One of the reasons is that the staysail helps the main and the mainsail helps the spinnaker and the interaction between the different sails increases their collective efficiency beyond that of the sum of the components. The most obvious effect is that of the headsail upon the flow over the leeside of the mainsail which can easily be seen by sticking cotton tell-tales over the leeside of the main. It may also be equally revealing in a tight duel with a similar boat on the wind to observe the effect of sending one of the larger crew members to stand in the slot. Wind-tunnel tests and experiments on full-sized yachts in ideal conditions reveal some less obvious aspects of the interplay of headsails and mainsails. The heeling force of a given area of the headsail, for example, is only about one-fifth of that of the mainsail. The genoa sheeting angle on the other hand does not affect heeling force but if set too hard can cause a severe decrease in the drive force. Almost the reverse obtains with the mainsail sheet – it has little effect upon the drive force but a great deal on the heel force. Overlap of mainsail by the headsail helps to smooth the flow and further improvements result if the camber of the headsail at the overlap is less than that of the main and the air flow in the slot is thereby speeded up by creating what is known as a 'venturi'.

One of the most interesting results from scientific analysis is that the best genoa sheeting angle for sailing to windward is not less than about $17\frac{1}{2}°$. (Sheeting angle in this instance means the angle which the chord of the foot of the genoa makes to the centre line of the hull.) This would presuppose that the hull has sufficient beam to provide mounting for the foresail fairleads to give this width of sheeting base and means that the optimum length/beam ratio should not be higher than about $3 \cdot 2 : 1$. As we saw in the last chapter, modern design favours length/beam ratios of this order or lower and, furthermore, since the beam for large headsails has to be well aft to provide the sheeting base, the wedge is more favoured than the 'cod's head mackerel tail' form for sheeting – base reasons alone. Smaller head sails of the jib-type where there is little or no overlap with the mainsail work best to windward with sheeting angles of about $10°$ or less and this accounts for the toe stubbing pair of fairleads sometimes found amidships on the deck of modern yachts.

Most yachtsmen appreciate the importance of a tight forestay for windward sailing and it is usual nowadays for the backstay bottle screw to be provided with a wheel and screw thread adjustment so that the forestay can be tightened on the wind and slacked off when reaching or running. Slackness in the forestay causes the headsail camber to increase and hence increases backwinding further along the mainsail. The greater camber also increases the minimum angle of incidence and hence a larger angle to the wind when beating. Also, the more camber the greater the heeling force. Off the wind increased camber in the headsail is of some advantage until that sail is eventually blanketed by the main. The spinnaker then comes into its own and the combination of mainsail plus spinnaker has been shown to have twice the drag of the same area of spinnaker. This is believed to be because the mainsail acts as a scoop and feeds air into the spinnaker at a higher velocity than would result were the spinnaker being flown on its own.

So far we have been dealing with single-masted sail plans of the sloop type and I should also remind you again that we have very largely also been dealing with the performance of the sail plan divorced from the hull. Before we look at two-masted and other unusual rigs, let us mate the hull and sails together again and consider the problem of hull and sail balance.

By 'balance' we mean satisfactory directional stability in a yacht – the quality of requiring little helm to maintain a straight course regardless of the yacht's attitude, conditions, sail plan or speed. Badly balanced yachts are difficult to sail and very tiring on the helmsman and in severe conditions can be dangerous, going 'hog-wild' on the helm and either going into uncontrollable broaches or equally uncontrollable gybes. Such erratic behaviour, apart from the risks to sails and gear, is fatal to good racing performance. Its occasional appearance is however one of the penalties we pay for high performance to windward in modern yachts and the high aspect ratio hull and sail profiles that this entails. It may be likened to a tendency among some of the more advanced designs of aircraft to be intolerant of high angles of incidence.

Although it is difficult to design a 'balanced' yacht, with certainty, fortunately many of the less desirable characteristics of unbalance can be eliminated by careful 'tuning' or at worst, adjustment to mast position or to the fitting of the rudder. The balance of a yacht depends upon both hull and sail factors and it is not until the complete assembly has been tested at sea that the characteristics of balance can be determined with any accuracy.

The mechanism of 'balance' or unbalance depends upon the relative movement of two important centres of pressure: the centre of lateral resistance of the hull (CLR) and the centre of effort of the sail plan (CE). When CE is directly above CLR the total sail force R_a and the total water force R_w from Fig 11 are acting along the same line – ignoring for the moment problems of heel – and there is no 'couple' attempting to turn the yacht's head. If CE is forward of CLR, however, there is a couple attempting to turn the yacht's head to leeward which the helmsman corrects by applying lee helm. Similarly if CE is aft of CLR there is a couple attempting to turn the yacht's head to windward which is corrected by weather helm. In both cases the adjustment to the 'unbalanced' condition is provided by the rudder which itself provides a significant proportion of the total lateral resistance. If the helm is pulled to weather the CLR is moved aft because the rudder, as it were, increases its share of the 'lift' or lateral resistance. If lee helm is applied the rudder produces, in effect, less lift and hence the CLR tends to move forward. In fact, the 'perfectly balanced boat' where the helmsman feels neither weather nor lee helm – the sort of yacht where the helm can be left – is not fully efficient because the rudder is not contributing to the generation of lateral resistance. This, of course, is inimical to good performance to windward and most yachts perform best when there is a small amount of weather helm. Tank tests have shown that 1° of weather helm shifts the CLR aft by 1–2 per cent of LWL, reducing leeway angle by about $\frac{1}{4}$° without any measurable increase in drag.

The positions of CLR and CE can be established within practical limits taking the geometric centre of the areas involved. Where there is more than one area – fin and rudder, jib and mainsail – it will be necessary to make adjustments for relative areas. In the case of sails, for example, the CE will lie on a line joining the geometric centres of the respective sails. Its position will however be determined by the proportion of the sail areas involved and also their efficiency. Foresails are usually given a factor of two for this reason, whereas mainsails are given a factor of one and mizzens a factor of 0·5.

As this method of measurement assumes that all the sails are trimmed flat, this is a static exercise and serves to give the designer an approximate position for the two centres so that he can give a 'lead' of CE against CLR by an amount based on his previous experience with similar designs. This amount is small – of the order of 1 or 2 per cent LWL – and the designer expects to achieve his final balance by adjustments to the rigging during sailing trials.

I have already mentioned the tendency for modern weatherly yachts to become unstable in direction when off the wind. The main causes here are the greater sailing speeds involved and the relative effects of wind gusts. From the previous chapter you will recall that when a hull is close to its maximum speed, it has a naturally greater bow-wave and hence an increased draught forward which, of course, brings CLR forward. At the same time the CE tends to move further outboard along the line of the boom and thus creates a turning couple in the athwartships plane. The effects of this couple become particularly marked when a gust strikes the yacht. Whereas the effect of a sudden increase in wind velocity – which is what a gust is – upon a close-hauled yacht is largely absorbed by an increase in heel, the broad reaching or running yacht endeavours to accelerate with the consequent effects upon her fore-and-aft trim and wave train. These and their attendant relative movements of CE and CLR produce very powerful turning couples particularly in a seaway which the rudder – or the helmsman – may lack the power to correct. The result can then be a swoop to windward ending in a broach as the boom digs in.

Modern design has produced two solutions to the problem of downwind directional stability. The first is the tendency to mount the rudder separately and well aft – thus moving CLR aft and making steering easier. The second is to mount the rudder on a skeg. This constitutes an increase in effective rudder area and improves the efficiency of the rudder by directing the water flow on to it. There is, inevitably, some increase in drag especially from skin-friction because wetted surface is increased, but, as a glance at Fig 1 on page 15 will show, most designers nowadays believe the benefits of directional stability outweigh the price of increased drag. As we have seen, not the least of these benefits is the ability to carry very large headsails and spinnakers on the close reach and this is yet another example of the interdependence of hull and sail plan.

In addition to the sails, however, the hull, especially when heeled, is 'offered' to the wind and aerodynamic forces result – largely drag forces. This drag, which results from the action of the wind on the hull above the waterline, the mast and rigging and exposed crew, is usually known as 'parasite drag' in that although unavoidable, it contributes virtually nothing to performance. There may be some slight help when off the wind, but on the wind, 'parasite drag' is a definite handicap. Looking at modern scientific designs, therefore, we find increasing attempts made to reduce parasite drag to a minimum particularly when the hull is heeled. Here, however, the modern predilection for high freeboard exacts a price in additional windage and *Noreyma*, for example, offers in relation to her sail area probably three times as much windage as would *Jolie Brise*. Where modern yachts have gained is in the reduction of windage from masts and rigging. Flush decks, streamlined deck houses, 'ant hills' and fittings, tumblehome and 'knuckles' all serve to smooth the flow over the heeled hull but these are only partially successful. The ability to carry sail, seaworthiness, crew comfort – to say nothing of the rating rule – all demand high freeboard. The price is significant windage and we are once again faced with conflicting demands that inevitably end in one of the many compromises that go to make up a yacht. All hull windage is however not lost because when close-hauled the 'intervention' of the hull between the boom and the water tends, if anything, to improve sail efficiency. This advantage disappears as the yacht bears away but this particu-

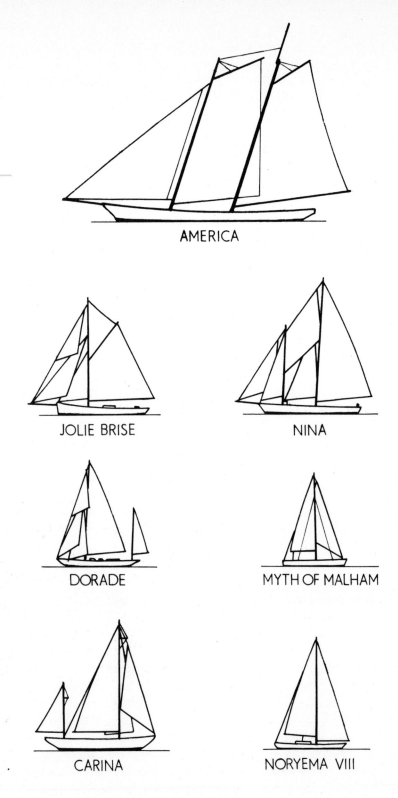

AMERICA

JOLIE BRISE

NINA

DORADE

MYTH OF MALHAM

CARINA

NORYEMA VIII

FIG 13   *The evolution of sail plans.*

Carina, *designed by Phil Rhodes and owned by Dick Nye, won the Fastnet in 1955 and 1957, and Class I in the 1959 Fastnet. Her performance under the* RORC *rule – she was a* CCA *yacht primarily – was one of the factors which caused many British owners to look across the Atlantic for their designers.*

Left: Blue Charm *designed by Illing-worth and Primrose in 1959, she had a remarkable light airs performance, probably as a result of the achievement of laminar flow over her under-body. She was no slouch in heavy weather either, and Dave Johnson began his offshore career by winning the Fastnet Inter-Regimental Cup in her in 1963.* Below: Casse Tête III. *A Swan 43 designed by Sparkman & Stephens and built by Nautor of Fin-land. She is typical of the series-built* GRP *production yachts which began to dominate the British offshore scene in the late sixties.*

TABLE I. The evolution of windward ability

Factors	Early schooner (America)	Pilot cutter (Jolie Brise)	Purpose-designed schooner (Dorade)	Post-war ocean-racer (Myth of Malham)	1972 'One-off'
Sail factors					
Sail Plan	Gaff	Gaff	Bermuda	Bermuda	Bermuda
Aspect ratio (luff/foot)	1:1	1:1	2:1	2·5:1	3:1
Rigging	Wire, hemp, handy-billy Much windage	–do–	Steel wire, levers and winches Some windage	Mechanically perfect, windage reduced	Marked effort to minimal windage
Sail leakage	Mast hoops Brailing to boom	–do–	Track and slides boom and mast external	Similar	Tracking slotted and shrouded
Sail material	Machine woven cotton	Canvas	Canvas	Canvas	Terylene Sealed stitching
Sail and Hull					
Power to Weight (SA/W$^{\frac{1}{3}}$)	190	179	190	165	180
Ability to carry sail*	Reef at Force 4	Reef at Force 5	Reef at Force 6	Reef at Force 7	Reef at Force 7
Hull factors					
Length/beam ratio	4:1	3:1	3·5:1	3·6:1	2·9:1
Ballast ratio	32%	30%	35%	51%	47%
Keel shape	Peripheral	Peripheral	Semi-elliptical	Trapezoid	Elliptical-fin
Keel aspect ratio§	0·30	0·40	0·60	0·90	1·20
Surface finish	Black varnish†	Black varnish		Hard racing	Polyurethane copper on GRP
Underbody	Red lead	Thick anti-fouling‡		Copper paint on on wood	

---

*   This can only be a general indication: much would depend upon sea state.

†   Black varnish was very prone to bubbling and blistering and was a compound of coal tar thinned with naptha.

‡   Thick anti-fouling paint required two men to put it on – one painting, the other stirring to keep it from setting. A smooth even finish was difficult to obtain.

§   Aspect ratio is calculated on basis of $\dfrac{\text{Draft}^2}{\text{Keel area}}$

lar effect explains the recent tendency to close the gap between boom and the foot of headsails and the surface of the sea by keeping them as low as possible.

In the last chapter we saw how hull drag tended to increase with increasing angle of heel but that in round figures, heel drag did not become significant until the heel angle exceeded 25°. Sails are also affected adversely by increasing angles of heel due to a combination of effects. The projected area 'seen' by the wind is reduced and as the wind blows increasingly upwards along the mast instead of across it, camber, aspect ratio, shape and angle of incidence all lose effectiveness. A heeled yacht is also affected by changes in incidence angle resulting from pitching and her ability to point is thereby reduced. Again, however, these effects are not of major significance at angles of heel up to about 25° and the lesson here for prudent skippers and crews is only too apparent!

Is it better to have one mast or two? This too tends to be something of a windage problem when performance is the governing factor. It used to be argued that yawls, schooners or ketches were less weatherly than sloops because their rigs tended to be of lower aspect ratio. This is no longer the case and the main difference between the sloops and yawls of today is that resulting from the effects of the windage of the extra mast and rigging when on the wind although, of course, even this can to some extent be reduced by ensuring that the mizzen pulls its weight to windward. Off the wind, the two-masted rig's ability to carry an additional staysail – and recall that staysails are twice as efficient as mainsails – is of considerable advantage both in terms of performance and to some extent in rating as we shall see in chapter 5. When racing performance is the sole consideration therefore the conditions most likely to be encountered are the dominant factors. Windward performance – such as is demanded in UK waters – calls for the sloop and high aspect ratio. Good downwind performance, such as is required in American waters and especially for the Honolulu Race – calls for low aspect ratio and the schooner, yawl or ketch. But don't be fooled. Nowadays the margins between rigs are small and since the war no less than four yawls have won the Fastnet.

Fig 13 shows how plans have evolved over the years and Table 1 explains how the figures for windward performance in chapter 1 were derived. Together they serve to demonstrate how applied scientific knowledge has slowly changed both the appearance and performance of the offshore yacht.

4
The Making
of the Yacht

In structural terms, all boats are in effect 'boxes' – odd-shaped boxes perhaps – but the basic construction of any vessel is that in which the sides, the deck and the bottom form the box regardless of the material of which the vessel is made. To be more precise, a vessel which floats on the restless sea is a box spar – to keep the nautical nomenclature – or a box section girder if we go back to basic engineering. As such it is subject to the strains of hogging and sagging which are applied to spars and girders in all situations. 'Hogging' occurs when a yacht is supported by a wave amidships whilst the ends are unsupported and tend to droop – like a hog. Sagging occurs when the yacht is supported at both ends – as when sailing at $V_s = 1\cdot34/\text{LWL}^{\frac{1}{2}}$ – with the middle unsupported so that the tendency is for it to sag like a sway-backed horse. (The modern term here is 'banana boat' which occurs when the ends tend to rise against the middle to the point when the forestay cannot be effectively tightened. It is, regrettably, a condition not unknown to hard-driven and 'blown' ocean-racers.) That the yacht shall be built to resist these strains and those in the way of the mast and the shrouds and at the ballast keel attachments is largely a matter of ensuring adequate strength in her keel, frames, deck and skin. Put another way it means that, bearing in mind the materials used and their inherent bending and breaking strain, the dimensions – usually called the 'scantlings' – of the various elements are adequate.

The usual practice is to employ a reliable set of scantling tables. These state a particular dimension for each part of the yacht which will give the necessary strength to the whole ship assuming that the workmanship is satisfactory and the basic material sound. For wooden yachts there are many time-honoured 'scantling' rules that have resulted from the accumulated experience over many years of outstanding designers. In the United States, the best-known scantling rules are 'Nevins' and 'Herreshoff's' both of which concern wooden yachts. In France there is the 'Bureau Veritas'. The proverbial symbol of perfection, however, is, and remains, 'Lloyd's' – that is Lloyd's Register of Shipping which covers all methods of yacht construction from traditional timber to 'glass reinforced plastic' (GRP).

'A 1 at Lloyd's and copper-bottomed' is an expression of general well-found seaworthiness that has made its way into common parlance as a synonym of general fitness and well being. We are not perhaps so concerned nowadays as they were in the seventeenth century when the saying originated, about being 'copper-bottomed' unless we are taking a wooden yacht into tropical teredo-infested waters for a long period. The 'A1 at Lloyd's', however, still obtains as a symbol of what is the best in yacht construction. One hears criticism from time to time that Lloyd's are too conservative and that the size of their standard scantlings is too heavy for modern purposes and offers too great a reserve of strength. Lloyd's Rules are however revised at regular intervals – the last time was in 1966 – to take account of developments in technique and even if a yacht is not 'classified', it would be unusual for the specification not to indicate at some point that key parts of the yacht at least were to be 'built to Lloyd's'.

Lloyd's Rules cover virtually everything that goes into the building of a yacht from the type and quality of the materials employed and the standard of workmanship to the machinery and the equipment down to the size of the anchor chain. The class 100 A 1 yacht – and several sub-divisions of this symbol of excellence – is virtually supervised by Lloyd's from the moment of conception when the drawings have to be submitted for approval. Thereafter the yacht is surveyed at intervals throughout her construction and any work not done in accordance with the Society's Rule or any material not up to Lloyd's standards has to be replaced. These surveys continue until the yacht is in the water when '. . . the yacht is to be examined afloat, and trials of the machinery are to be conducted . . . Sails are to be hoisted and checked'. Surveys continue throughout the life of the yacht if she is to retain her classification at two-yearly intervals with 'special surveys every four years'. In this way, Lloyd's 100 A 1 retains its world-wide credibility – the New York Yacht Club adopted Lloyd's standards in 1928 – as a hall-mark of all that is best in a yacht. In many cases, national rules for construction are based on commercial ship practices and unsuitable for yachts and Lloyd's provides the only valid guidance. Lloyd's Rules for steel yachts are a particular case in point.

In this chapter we shall be looking at the standards of the various scantlings required by the Lloyd's Rules for yachts built in the usual modern materials – natural timber, moulded plywood, steel, light alloy and fibreglass.

It would be as well to remind ourselves briefly first of the main elements of a traditionally constructed yacht's hull and the function of the various parts in ensuring that the hull withstands the stresses and strains it will encounter from a sea that recognises no standards – not even Lloyd's.

Fig 14 shows the main components of a yacht's anatomy. For convenience we can group them together into the following: the keel, the frames, the floors, the longitudinals, the outer skin, the deck planking and the beams. And holding everything together – the all-important fastenings.

The keel comprises the heavy timbers of the wood keel, the stem, the stern post and the deadwood and counter timbers – the centre-line structure. This is effectively the backbone of the yacht and from it spring the frames like the 'ribs' they are usually called in stock newspaper phrases. Holding the frames in place on the keel, and preventing them from springing apart, are the 'floors' – not of course to be confused with the cabin sole which usually hides them from view. At the other end of the frames is the longitudinal beam-shelf which also serves as mounting for the deck beams and, quite frequently, the deck beams and the beam-shelf and the frames are linked together by hanging knees especially where there is extra strain upon the deck as in way of the mast. In addition to the beam-shelf, the other longitudinals are bilge stringers – usually found nowadays only in larger yachts – and the carlings of hatchways and coachroof. This framework is then clad with planking and decking and these in themselves contribute the major portion of the strength of the hull. They also contribute the greatest single weight – apart from the ballast keel – in a yacht's structure, amounting to around 15 per cent of the bare wood hull.

Basically what we are looking for in a yacht if we are to achieve the optimum performance is the maximum structural strength for the minimum structural weight. Taking weight first, in round figures the total displacement of a modern yacht is made up of weights in the following rough proportions:

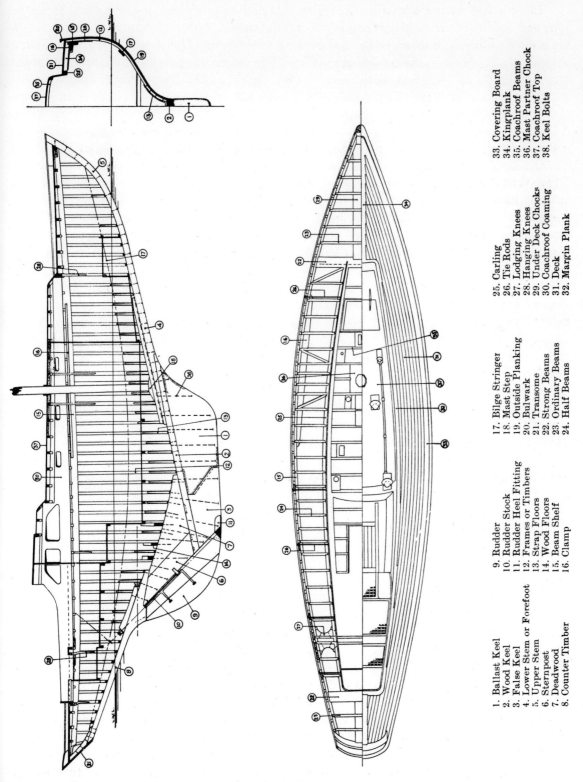

1. Ballast Keel
2. Wood Keel
3. False Keel
4. Lower Stem or Forefoot
5. Upper Stem
6. Sternpost
7. Deadwood
8. Counter Timber

9. Rudder
10. Rudder Stock
11. Rudder Heel Fitting
12. Frames or Timbers
13. Strap Floors
14. Wood Floors
15. Beam Shelf
16. Clamp

17. Bilge Stringer
18. Mast Step
19. Outside Planking
20. Bulwark
21. Transome
22. Strong Beams
23. Ordinary Beams
24. Half Beams

25. Carling
26. Tie Rods
27. Lodging Knees
28. Hanging Knees
29. Under Deck Chocks
30. Coachroof Coaming
31. Deck
32. Margin Plank

33. Covering Board
34. Kingplank
35. Coachroof Beams
36. Mast Partner Chock
37. Coachroof Top
38. Keel Bolts

FIG 14   *Components of a traditional wooden hull.*

Ballast	40–45%
Hull structure	30–40%
Accommodation, gear, auxiliary engine, masts, sails, crew, fuel, water, etc	20–30%

What we are discussing here is the 'live weight' of the yacht when it is actually in the water and eager for the sea. In this condition the actual displacement will probably exceed the design displacement by a fair margin. In my experience, the ocean-racing load usually puts a 30 ft yacht down by about $1\frac{1}{2}$ in – probably somewhere about an extra ton. The range of values I have given don't add up to 100 per cent. They are, of course, dependent variables. If we have a heavy hull structure we shall have to reduce the ballast ratio to carry the same gear and accommodation if we don't want to increase the displacement. On the other hand, if we want a high ballast-ratio, we may have to cut back the scale of accommodation and load.

Further, recalling the relationship between displacement and sail area – our fundamental power/weight ratio – if we increase displacement we need also to increase sail area to maintain performance. In the larger yachts this could mean a sizeable increase in weight if an extra hand is needed to handle the sails. There is himself, his kit, his food and drink, his bunk – and so on. Once again, we see the compromise between conflicting requirements that goes to make up a yacht. When a hull is being designed the type of construction to be used has to be decided very early. If the owner wants traditional planking, interior panelling in teak and a 'laid and paid' deck, all at Lloyd's, then heavy displacement is unavoidable. If he prefers steel then displacement can be moderate. Light displacement goes with cold-moulded plywood, aluminium alloy and fibre-glass – or, of course, you could settle for a bigger yacht. In all respects, you pays your money and takes your choice.

Let's toss all these variables into the melting pot and see what differing combinations are possible. Leaving aside for the moment those two important considerations of cost and rating, let us assume that an owner wants a one-off cruiser-racer of around 27 ft LWL – for the One Ton Cup perhaps – and is prepared to build in any of the accepted methods. Let us also assume that for rating reasons and the type of sailing the owner will be doing, the designer thinks that a length/weight ratio of about 300 and a sail/displacement ratio of about 180 should be aimed at. The designer's blotting pad arithmetic might then look like the table opposite.

This is of course a slightly unreal situation because most designers tend to specialise in methods of construction and it is unlikely that any owner would be faced with so wide a choice. Nonetheless, the Table serves to illustrate the influence that methods of construction can have upon displacement. In practice, too, the figures used are also slightly unreal. The weight of the wood hull for example would depend upon the type of timber used, whether there was a laid deck or a plywood deck and to what extent the construction used steel or other metal members – what is known as a composite hull. It would also depend on how lavish were the fittings and furnishings below decks which could easily add another ton to the final weight if much teak were used. In the cold-moulded plywood hull, essentially a light displacement form of construction, weight would undoubtedly be saved by spartan furnishing and a lighter auxiliary and the same is true of the alloy and GRP hulls. This in turn would probably mean some saving in sail area and hence in the weight of mast, sails and rigging.

LWL 27ft

Construction	Wood to Lloyd's	Cold-moulded plywood	Welded steel	Welded alloy	GRP
Weight of hull structure	2·10	1·60	2·50	1·60	1·70
Hull and deck fittings	0·25	0·25	0·25	0·25	0·25
Accommodation and furnishing	0·40	0·40	0·40	0·30	0·20*
Mast and Sails and Rigging	0·50	0·50	0·50	0·50	0·50
Auxiliary engine	0·50	0·50	0·50	0·50	0·50
Crew, kit and stores	0·70	0·70	0·70	0·70	0·70
Bare hull weight	4·45	3·95	4·85	3·85	3·85
Ballast at 45%	3·65	3·25	3·25*	3·15	3·15
Displacement	8·10	7·20	8·10	7·00	7·00
Length/weight ratio $\left(\dfrac{W}{L}/100\right)^3$	270	250	270	233	233
Sail area/weight ratio = 180	720 ft²	687 ft²	720 ft²	660 ft²	660 ft²

* This ballast ratio is 40% – the reduction is possible in steel yachts because of the weight of the floors and bottom plating.

Fanatics would say, too, that an allowance for five men of 300 lb a man was lavish in the extreme. As Captain John Illingworth is reputed once to have said, the ideal ocean racer is an open box. You fill it with straw at the start of the race. When the crew are hungry they eat it; when they are tired they sleep in it and you muck the boat out like a stable when back on moorings.

The welded steel form of construction means, usually, that to keep displacement moderate, the ballast ratio has to be reduced and this is acceptable because of the heavy weight of the steel floors and bottom plating which serve as ballast in themselves. Finally, as we shall see, the term 'GRP' is as generic as 'timber' and hulls of this size have been built as light as 1,000 lb. (The figures in brackets in the preceding Table indicate the more likely adjusted values of the various items and the final outcome.) As I said this is blotting-pad thinking with a pencil staff, and for drill purposes only.

So much then for weight. We now have to consider strength. And weight is not necessarily proportional to strength. Indeed of the boats in the Table, there is probably little to choose between them on the score of strength although each may be stronger in a subtly different way. Personally, my money will always be on cold-moulded plywood because I survived being run down by a tanker in the North Sea some years ago in a cold-moulded plywood yacht and afterwards we calculated that with a yacht of any other form of construction we should have sunk like a stone: wood, because the planks would have sprung below the waterline; steel, because the thin plating would undoubtedly have been pierced through; and glass-fibre, because the deck would have been separated from the hull at the first impact. As it was, we escaped with a weeping gash in the topsides and that was all. But fortunately, even in the crowded waters of the English Channel or Long Island Sound, collisions with tankers are mercifully rare and the ever present destructive force is the power of the sea alone.

Despite the popularity of GRP construction and the ever-growing numbers of series-built production yachts in that material, natural timber maintains high popularity for the construction of yachts of all types. For wood is still a superb material to work with and the best of it possesses as high a strength/weight ratio as mild steel. However, to achieve the vital strength in a hull, the scantlings must be adequate and the fastenings reliable. Lloyd's, as we have previously mentioned, lay down values for the scantlings of each of the major hull components for various methods of construction and types of wood. They are also specific on the type and materials of the fastenings used – a yacht, in other words, floats not only on its timbers but more on its keel bolts and nails.

The rigidity of the hull and its main resistance to sagging and hogging is provided by the centreline structure. This comprises the wood keel, stem, stern post and counter timbers. For a boat of the size we have been considering, 27 ft LWL, Lloyd's would call for these to be of timber weighing not less than 40 lb/ft³ – teak, for example, weighs 41 lb/ft³, English oak, 45 lb and the scantlings would be 4 in by 8 in. For frames, the requirement is for timber of 45 lb/ft³ and the scantlings depend on whether the frames are 'grown', 'bent', or laminated. Frames cut from the solid wood to the shape required are known as 'grown' or 'sawn'; 'bent' 'steamed' frames are cut straight and bent to the desired shape in a steam kiln. Laminated frames – of both types – have to conform in weight to the solid timber form and comply with the specifications for glues. There are also steel frames and Lloyd's also accept combinations of grown, bent, steel and laminated frames and the scantlings and spacings between successive frames vary according to the mixture. For example, for our 27 ft LWL yacht, the size and spacings would be these:

	Cross-section (in²)	Spacing (in)
All bent	3·65	8½
All grown	7·50	12
Laminated	5	12
All steel	2×2×0·20 (0·8 in²)	12

Hull planking, beam shelves, bilge stringers, deck beams and knees and coachroof coamings are required to be of timber at 35 lb/ft³. The sectional area of the beam-shelf would be about 7½ in² and the bilge stringer 6 in² although the latter can be dispensed with in smaller craft except where bent frames are used in preponderance. Hull planking would be ⅞ in thick but this can be reduced if the yacht is clencher (clinker) built, has a double diagonal skin or one of the cold-moulded laminates. Single-skin plywood hulls – assuming that an acceptable grade of plywood is used and that the basic framing is adequate – can be 25 per cent thinner, i.e. down to about ⅝ in. Similarly, the thickness of decking (where a timber weight of 27 lb/ft³ is called for) can be reduced from the standard ⅞ in thickness; if heavier timber like teak is used or again, suitable plywood when the thickness can in the case of decks be reduced by 30 per cent or less than ½ in.

We shall be comparing these timber scantlings with other modern forms of construction later but, glancing backwards, it is interesting to see how over the years, Lloyd's has reflected the tendency towards lighter construction in yachts.

	Pre-war	1950	1957	1966
Keel	4½×10	4½×9	4½×9	4×8
Beam-shelf (area)	11	9½	9½	7½
Bilge stringer-area	8	8	7	Needed only with all bent frames – 6
Outside planking	1·20	1	1	0·88
Deck P	1·10	1	1	0·88
Bent frames	Not allowed	8	8	9·125

These figures may not seem particularly significant in themselves but the saving on the thickness of decks and planking alone could amount to a 3 or 4 per cent saving on the hull structure weight. Accompanying these changes in scantlings for the 'classic' wooden yacht has been the steady acceptance of new methods and new materials by the Society and, indeed, one might argue that until a new method of yacht construction has had the approval of Lloyd's it must remain at least slightly suspect. Before World War II, Lloyd's had two sets of scantling rules – one, the heavier, for cruising yachts known as the 'A' class, the other for the Metre Class of inshore racers known as the 'R' class. After a review of the rules in 1948, both classes were merged and the scantlings were reduced for all classes down to those of the 'R' class. The rules were revised again in 1954 and 1957 but it is not until the last 1966 revision that there is any mention of either marine plywood or the cold-moulded method of construction. On the other hand, Lloyd's classified the first reinforced plastic hull in 1956 and issued 'Provisional Rules for the Construction of Reinforced Plastic Yachts' in 1961. With some slight editorial amendments these rules are in force today – and are still provisional. The rules for steel yachts naturally evolved from Lloyd's long experience with steel ships. It is also worth observing here that the 1966 rules make provision for the first time for Class 100 A 1 catamaran and 100 A 1 trimaran.

The Dutch, with their long experience of building small craft of all types for use on their canals coupled with the virtual absence of timber in Holland, have become the leaders in the building of welded steel hulls for yachts. The major difficulty is in ensuring that the thin plating used (3 mm) is not subject to distortion and that the hulls have a fair even finish. Part of the secret lies in the sequence of welding – if the deck is welded before the topsides, for example, it is not unknown for the shrinkage to lift the bow and stern of the vessel and throw propeller shaft out of line. The rest is involved in using the minimum amount of welding between the steel shell and the frames and a great deal of careful stretching and coaxing like that practised by automobile panel-beaters the world over. Apart from its great strength, the small size of frames and other structures and the ability to build-in tanks and the like, one of the advantages of steel construction is the amount of room it provides for a given waterline length. Against this, we have already seen the weight problem and there is also the self-evident one of corrosion although modern techniques have tended to make this less of a bug-bear than it was a generation ago.

Cold-moulded construction is a process of building up a series of layers of veneer laid diagonally in strips over a wooden mould of the hull. Lloyd's Rules require that the veneers shall be from suitable timbers – both the mahoganies and makore and Honduras cedar are included in the 'most suitable group' – and that the strips shall not be wider than 5 in or thicker than 3·5 mm. Special attention has also to be paid to the glue used and in meeting the requirement of maintaining the correct temperature when using it. The glue has to be of resorcinol or phenolic type and must meet a WBP (Water and Boil Proof) specification. As evidence of the basic structural strength of a cold-moulded skin, Lloyd's permit either a 10 per cent reduction of thickness compared with natural timber and a 25 per cent reduction of frame scantlings or, with standard framing, a 25 per cent reduction in skin thickness. This immediately indicates the potential of this form of construction for the light displacement type.

The acme of light displacement construction is aluminium alloy. This material, which has now been developed in a form which completely overcomes all its former problems of corrosion in salt water, is gaining rapidly in popularity in the United States. Building techniques are similar to those used in wood. A thin aluminium skin is wrapped around a skeleton of supporting frames and stringers. As in aircraft construction, however, aluminium boats have many more longitudinal members than do wooden yachts. The skin is then either plated with plates shaped to meet the designed shapes of the hull – a complex and difficult task – or stretch-formed by use of dies and a press. This latter process, which is common aircraft practice, is particularly suited to mass production, but the machinery involved is immense and highly expensive. (From the United States I have, however, seen suggestions that boat builders will in time be able to share presses with aircraft manufacturers to keep costs down.) Some aluminium yachts have the same thickness of plate throughout the hull – $\frac{3}{16}$ in is a much favoured thickness but others, as Lloyd's stipulate, vary the thickness of the plating throughout the hull. In areas where there is extra stress – in way of the keel and the mast – the thickness of the plating increases to as much as $\frac{3}{8}$ in.

Aluminium hulls either stretch-formed or welded can be as smooth in finish as wood or fibreglass, and although such hulls have a reputation for being noisy, suitably applied foam compounds at critical areas – like the lining of the mast for example – can cut down the noise. The main snag with aluminium which is likely to persist is that of cost. Although in series production aluminium hulls could be competitive with either wood or fibreglass in the small sizes – dinghies and runabouts – as soon as complex curves are involved, the glass-fibre process is simpler and cheaper. When, however, we come to the larger-sized one-off yachts, many American authorities now favour aluminium. *Carina* (a direct descendant of the Fastnet winner of the 1950s) won the Bermuda in 1970 and was made of aluminium alloy.

Although Lloyd's Rules for the construction of reinforced plastic yachts are provisional, the vast majority of sea-going yacht hulls moulded in the UK are to the Lloyd's specification. All the major GRP moulding manufacturers are on the Lloyd's approved list which involves the Society's approval of the works and the supervision of its inspectors. The buildings are required to provide adequate heating, insulation and ventilation to ensure that conditions are suitable for the resins being used. The scantling rule is based on the use of an unsaturated polyester-resin system with glass-fibre reinforcements and moulded by the contact or hand lay-up process against a male or female mould. Lloyd's specify the types of polyester-resin catalyst and accelerator to be used and the thickness of the glass-fibre reinforcement – 1 oz chopped strand mat being the norm. The resin-to-glass ratio is specified for the hand lay-up process at not less than $2\frac{1}{2}$:1 nor greater than 3:1 by weight. This is assumed to give the laminate a tensile strength of 12,000–14,000 psi which is about the same as teak. The scantlings are then given in tables in two forms. Those for the skin are given in weights of glass per square foot of laminate – a yacht of 30 ft length for example would have '9 oz' topsides (about $\frac{1}{4}$ in thick). The scantlings of stiffening which GRP construction requires either in the form of in-moulded angular glass sections or light alloy sections often of the well-known 'top-hat section' are given as 'moduli'. This is a measure of the volume of actual material in the sides (webs) and the face area of the stiffeners.

GRP has many advantages for yacht construction – and not a few disadvantages. It makes for lightness in hull construction and, as we have seen, lends itself readily to series production methods. It has a low modulus of elasticity (see Table 2) which means that it has a high resistance to shock loads: planing power boat hulls are one example, pulling dinghies regularly dropped from the deck into the sea are another. It requires joins and angles in construction to be rounded, however, and, in general, flat surfaces have to be avoided unless strongly supported. Again, GRP gets harder with age and tends to craze so that it begins to look unattractive and may even add to surface friction. It is also subject to abrasion and once the outer 'gel' layer has been eroded, it quickly collects dirt and looks ugly. On the other hand, a combination of GRP and teak or mahogany-veneered plywood can easily keep things ship-

TABLE 2.   **Strengths of materials and scantlings to Lloyd's Rules (L = 30ft)**

Material	Mild steel	Aluminium alloy	GRP	Teak
Ultimate tensile strength (lb/in²)	67,200	33/40,000	12/14,000	15,000
Modulus of elasticity ($\times 10^6$)	30	10	0·9 – 1·2	2·4
Weight/ft³	490 lb	169 lb	107 lb	45 lb
Scantlings *Shell*				
— above LWL	0·137 in (3,5 mm)*	0·19 in (4,8 mm)	0·33 in (8,3)	0·875 in (22 mm)
— below LWL	0·165 in (4,2 mm)	0·38 in (9,4 mm)	0·25 in (0·64)	0·875 in (22 mm)
Frames	2 in × 1½ in × 0·18 in		2·4 in³†	2¼ × 1⅛
—spacing	15 in		17 in	8·5 in
Deck	0·125 in (3,2 mm)	0·16 in (3,9 mm)	0·33 in (8,3)	0·875 in (22 mm)

* The scantlings given for mild steel plate are largely theoretical minimum values and may require the use of specially rolled plate or of over-thick stock sizes.

† This is the modulus for the framing. The actual dimensions of the frames – or more correctly stiffeners – depend on the shape: face area and depth. For a 'top hat' shape the optimum depth would be about 2 in with a face area of 1 in.

shape. Indeed, taken all round, it is hardly surprising that something like 80 per cent of all new yachts built are of GRP construction.

Before we leave the question of hull construction and the relative strengths of materials, let us look briefly at the relative strengths of the comparative scantlings of a 30 ft yacht in wood (teak), cold-moulded plywood, aluminium alloy, welded steel and GRP as laid down by Lloyd's (see Table 2 on previous page).

So much then for hulls. Before we leave the subject of construction we should look at two other aspects which can have implications upon performance and behaviour in a seaway: the mast and its rigging; the engines and its propeller.

Although, as we have seen, Lloyd's lay down detailed and precise scantlings for the hull structure, they do not offer any specification for masts and rigging. The short answer is that whereas the stresses and strains upon a hull can be calculated within reasonable limits, those upon the mast and rigging involve so many variables and so many broad assumptions as to be beyond codification. Some people – especially with the aid of computers – attempt to calculate mast scantlings; others 'study successful spars and forget the mathematics', as Frances Herreshoff, one of America's greatest designers and himself father of a scantling code, once put it. But masts still break for reasons nobody expects – metal fatigue, problems of lifeing materials, and the like, are recent examples. Extruded alloy sections, of which there is an enormous selection, are now the normal fit in all types of yachts from day-boats to the biggest ocean-racers. They offer a number of advantages over masts in wood. At the same weight they are stronger or at the same strength they are lighter (an echo of the hull situation) or they can have smaller dimensions and simpler staying. The whole thrust of modern mast design has been towards saving weight and windage aloft and keeping a straight leading edge on the main and the genoa. This has been achieved by lighter stronger masts and the use of the minimum of spreaders, jumper struts and runner backstays. As far as is practicable, running rigging is contained within the mast. What the ancients thought of *America*, as we saw in chapter 1, was that she had 'two noble sticks, without an extra rope'. We have come a long way since then in both the nobility of sticks and the elimination of rope, but there is a long way still to go, as we shall see in chapter 7.

The engine propeller assembly in a sailing yacht provides auxiliary power, an element of ballast and very frequently considerable and unnecessary hull drag when proceeding 'by the action of the wind upon the sails' rather than that of the mixture upon the pistons. Taking the power requirement first, the calculations of the power of the engines required are reasonably straightforward. With tides in coastal waters averaging up to $3\frac{1}{2}$ knots, there is little point in fitting a motor that will not get a yacht over the tide in the worst circumstances. For all practical purposes this means a minimum of 6 knots in yachts of all sizes from day-boats to massive cruisers. A rough rule of thumb – and probably as accurate as a page of calculations – is that 1 hp/ton of displacement will give a speed/length ratio of unity. In other words, in a 36 ft yacht we can allow 1 hp/ton of displacement and achieve our 6 knots but in the smaller yachts we shall have to increase the horse-power/displacement ratio to as much as 2 hp/ton. The table on the facing page gives an indication of the engine horse-powers needed to make 6 knots in average yachts.

In practice it is clearly better to choose the nearest engine power above that required rather than the one below it. Extra power means a smaller throttle opening and hence less wear on the engine. This can be overdone, however, and, as we saw in chapter 2, above

$V/L^{\frac{1}{2}} = 1\cdot5$ the extra power is dissipated in climbing up the bow wave whether the power is natural or mechanical.

The average weight of an auxiliary engine with its gear box and other ancillaries is usually not much less than half a ton and in the larger sizes may be considerably more. Since in most yachts the auxiliary is used but occasionally it also has to earn its keep when silent – like the off-watch crew in an ocean-racer on the wind – by contributing to the stability of the ship. As with other ballast the optimum place is as low as possible and at the centre of gravity of the whole hull. For the best performance and easiest motion in a seaway it clearly pays to keep weights concentrated amidships. Equally important for the health of the engine is that it shall not be tilted beyond the maximum angle stipulated by the makers. The shafting has to be such to ensure that the propeller remains in the water even when the yacht is heeled and in practice this probably means somewhere between a third and a half of the draft. Nowadays, with the development of highly efficient flexible hydraulic drives, engine installation is much less of a problem than it used to be when a short straight run for the propeller shaft was the main criterion. The traditional position at the base of the companionway has now given way to the more usual position in or under the main saloon. In short you can, nowadays, put the auxiliary where it suits you for convenience, comfort or where you can get the most out of the rating rule. For this latter purpose it is by no means unknown for the engine to be mounted in the fore-peak with the prop shaft serving a dual purpose as a bracing bar in the loo.

LWL	W	$V/L^{\frac{1}{2}} = 6K$	HP
16	1·0	1·50	$1\frac{1}{2}$
20	1·5	1·35	2
25	3·0	1·20	$3\frac{1}{2}$
30	6·0	1·10	7
35	10·5	1·02	11
40	17·0	0·95	16
50	33·0	0·85	28
60	52·5	0·78	41

Propellers pose intricate problems in offshore racing yachts. In cruising yachts it is enough to decide on the size, type and installation of the propeller assembly necessary to obtain the best efficiency from the auxiliary and then to let the drag when sailing take care of itself by fitting a sailing clutch and letting the propeller rotate in the stream. This is frequently an adequate solution and is the one usually employed by motor sailers. It is not without its snags. A free-wheeling propeller is noisy and it also causes wear in the shaft bearings. Nor is the free-wheeling condition always that of minimum drag in all conditions of sailing. The propeller has for one thing to be able to rotate fast enough – the actual speed will vary from one propeller to another – and that means free bearings, well-greased glands and a smooth propeller.

For offshore racing yachts, the IOR has ruled that propellers must be stopped and locked whilst racing. In rating terms there is a great deal more to it than that and we shall be looking at the propeller rating factors in chapter 6. In design terms, leaving aside rating factors, the rule means that the selection of the type, size and installation of the propeller has to give priority to minimising the effects of a locked propeller upon sailing performance. For these can be considerable. The standard type of fixed three-bladed propeller – propellers like scantlings can be picked out from tables – for the horse-power of the type of auxiliary suitable for say a 40 ft LWL yacht (about 16–20 bhp) when stopped and locked could increase the total hull drag by as much as 35 per cent and no allowance under the rating rule is likely to compensate for an increase in drag of that order.

Although the drag of a locked propeller is clearly related to its size, it is the area of the blades which is important rather than the diameter. This means that choosing the smallest possible screw may not necessarily be the best answer because proportionately the blade area will be larger if the screw is to provide adequate performance under power. The problem here in a word is 'cavitation'. This is the condition when the propeller blades, which are akin to aerofoils and hydrofoils, fail to generate lift because the smooth flow of the water over them is disturbed. There are many causes for cavitation in auxiliary installations. The most frequent ones are propellers too small being operated at too high rpm and too close to the surface. In short the propeller under power threshes the water into a pother of foam while the yacht hardly moves forward at all. Contrariwise, this type of installation – a small diameter, low blade area screw just below the waterline – is that which is likely to produce the minimum drag under sail and the whole problem of achieving a satisfactory propeller installation for the offshore racing yacht lies in achieving a compromise between the two conflicting requirements. The IOR for its part has set the limits by insisting that if an engine and propeller are fitted they will only qualify for an allowance if they are capable of propelling the yacht at a speed equal to $0.75/L^{\frac{1}{2}} = $ say $4\frac{1}{2}$ knots in a 36 ft LOA yacht. (The IOR also, incidentally, does not permit propellers to be retracted when racing.) The effect of the IOR requirement means that the fitting of inefficient installations is precluded and no one thereby is likely to take an engine and propeller along for the ride just to gain rating advantage.

Hull characteristics also play their part in determining the type of propeller installation. In heavy displacement yachts it may be possible to install a propeller at an adequate depth without exposed shafting. With light displacement profiles it may be necessary to fit extensive shafting to get the propeller sufficiently clear of the hull to achieve an adequate diameter or to get it deep enough below the waterline. Propellers themselves come in a variety of types – fixed three-bladed; two-bladed folding or feathering, some with shafts and some with none. In terms of drag when sailing – and ignoring rating allowances – the order of merit for a propeller of the same radius is as follows:

Minimum drag:	Folding propeller without shafting
	Feathering propeller without shafting
Significant drag:	Folding propeller with shafting
	Feathering propeller with shafting
Serious drag:	Solid propeller without shafting
	Solid propeller with shafting

If we compare propellers of differing diameters the following figures give an idea of how type and size can vary for the same drag characteristics. The drag of a propeller and shafting installation will vary with the square of the speed, and if we take an installation giving say, a

r/V^2 factor of 0·55, i.e. 2·2 lb resistance at 2 knots, 13·5 at 5 knots and 55 lb at 10 knots, we would have a choice of:

Folding propeller without shafting of 4 ft diameter
Feathering propeller without shafting of 3 ft diameter
Folding with shafting of 2·5 ft
Feathering with shafting of 2 ft
Solid without shafting of 1·25 ft
Solid with shafting of 1 ft.

Or we could fit a 12 in folding propeller without shafting at negligible drag and still have a propeller suitable to drive us at $0·75/L$. But is this the best answer? In absolute terms it could well be the best answer, but we are dealing here with yachts operating under the IOR rating rule, and as we saw in chapter 1, rating rules dominate racing design to the point where absolutes invariably have to be qualified. The absolutes of propeller installations are no exception as we shall see in chapter 6.

5

Rating Rules and Races

Let us suppose that on the basis of what we have discussed so far in this book we were required to produce a formula which would enable us to assess the likely speed performance in given conditions of a particular yacht. From chapter 2 the obvious first parameter is that of sailing length which we will designate L leaving aside for the moment whether we mean LWL or LOA or points in between. From chapter 3 we would realise that whilst L was a predominant factor in determining speed, power-to-weight ratio would exert a major influence on whether the speed potential of a yacht's L could be realised. The formula here, you will recall, is $SA/W^{\frac{1}{3}}$, where SA is sail area and W is displacement. Displacement/length ratio could also be relevant. Putting these factors together we could say that a yacht's speed potential would be proportional to her sailing length multiplied by her sail-area/displacement ratio and we could then set out a formula something like this:

$$\text{Speed potential} \propto L(SA)/W^{\frac{1}{3}}$$

The first term takes care of the length/displacement factor so we need not include it further. Displacement (W) is difficult and expensive to measure in practice but it is a measure of volume as much as weight and is determined by '$L \times$ beam $\times$ depth' so we could substitute the awkward factor $\sqrt[3]{W}$ by the $\sqrt[3]{B \times D}$. Our formula would then look like this:

$$\text{Speed potential} = \frac{LSA^{\frac{1}{2}}}{BD^{\frac{1}{2}}}$$

Let us now look at what sort of a figure we would get from this by applying it to a real yacht – and who better than the Bermuda Cup winner *Noreyma* – but using rounded figures:

$$L = 40 \text{ ft}; \quad SA^{\frac{1}{2}} = 36; \quad BD^{\frac{1}{2}} = 9; \quad \text{speed potential} = 1600.$$

This is quite a meaningless figure, and to bring it back into relation with the sailing length L and make it a negotiable quantity as a function of the yacht's speed, we need to apply a constant. If in the example above we employ a factor of 0·20 then the result would be as follows:

$$\text{Rating in linear units} = 0{\cdot}20 \, \frac{(L/S^{\frac{1}{2}})}{BD^{\frac{1}{2}}}$$

$$\text{For } Noreyma \; VIII = \frac{0{\cdot}2 \times 40 \times 36}{9} = 32 \text{ ft}$$

Rocquette, later Bluejacket III, *designed in 1964 by Camper & Nicholson. She represents what might be seen as the last flowering of British native offshore racer design before the US deluge. Her clear virtually flush deck without benefit of coachroof was an innovation which has endured. Happily, the slab-sided doghouse has now virtually disappeared.*

Below: Noreyma VII *or VG. Designed by Dick Carter in 1969, she has an adjustable drop keel designed by Ron Amey himself, hence the 'variable geometry' connotation. She was moderately successful under the* RORC *rule, but the idea of varying the keel shape to suit the conditions may in due course make her a real pioneer of progress.*

Above: Noreyma VIII. *A Swan 48 designed in 1971 by Sparkman & Stephens and again built by Nautor. Note how the doghouse is faired into the virtually flush deck.*

And so we have a scientifically based formula which will give us a rational assessment of a yacht's potential speed under sail – in short, we have a rating rule. Indeed, as we shall see, this was the basis of the rating rule used by the Royal Ocean Racing Club from 1926 onwards when this very formula was used itself and further, that this formula still lies at the heart of the latest International Offshore Rule. But a formula is all we have got. Before we can use it to assess yachts of widely differing types so that they may race equitably against each other, we have two other requirements to meet. The first of these is to determine how to measure each of the basic factors taking into account the great variety of hull shapes and the plethora of rigs and sail plans. The second – and no less important – is having established a rational basis of measurement and a logical formula to convert measurement into rating, how to translate rating results into a handicap which will be fair to all comers. (We shall be looking into this aspect in the next chapter.)

'Being fair to all comers' – this idea in itself begs a massive number of questions. All comers are certain to include boats which were already in existence before the rule was devised, boats which will be built largely in ignorance of the rule and, in increasing numbers, boats which will be built specifically to take advantage of any loopholes in the rule and its effects upon design. Designers have a perfect right to do this provided their yachts are safe and seaworthy – and thereby hangs another tale: how do we ensure that the rule will 'encourage the design and building of yachts in which speed and seaworthiness are combined, without favouring any particular type'.

The answer is probably akin to that given to the American tourist who asked the gardeners in an Oxford college how they achieved such superb turf. 'You start with good seed then you waters, weeds and mows it every day for three hundred years . . .' A rating rule is much the same. You start with a rational formula and you trim it and you check it and you balance it until finally you get a 'universal rule' which ensures the ultimate objective is attained: the elimination of the yacht's performance itself from any yacht race so that skills of the crews alone may determine the outcome. When that day dawns – and three hundred years may well be par for the course – yacht designers and scientists will beg for their bread in the streets of Cowes, Lymington, New York and Sydney – and there will be no more sin.

Happily for them we are as yet only a mere third of the way down that particular fairway even if we count the Victorian experience in devising rules for inshore craft. If we stick to the offshore racing business, the history of the rating rule *per se* has not yet reached its half century. Nonetheless we have accumulated a great deal of experience under the related headings of formula; measurement; time allowance and design influence. Let us look into a little of it before we consider how best to 'water, weed and mow' the seed of a formula we planted earlier in this chapter.

Figure 15 is a summary of the major developments in rating rules over the last century or so. In many ways it is a chronicle of 'the state of the art' of yacht racing with all its ramifications in the field of design and construction and of the increasingly complicated legislation needed to keep the sport just and fair to all comers without stultifying its natural evolution. It also shows, I believe, the essential unity of the sport both geographically and across its own natural internal divisions. The current International Offshore Rule owes much to the Cruising Club of America Rule for details of measurement but its basic formula clearly stems from that of the Royal Ocean Racing Club which in turn evolved from Malden Heckstall Smith's Boat Racing Association formula. That in turn stemmed from the subtle union of two American rules – Nathaneal Herreshoff's Universal Rule and the Seawanhaka Rule, both of

FIG 15 *Table showing the evolution of the International Offshore Rating Rule.*

INSHORE RACING

DATES	RATING RULE	FORMULA	MEASUREMENT	TIME ALLOWANCE	DESIGN IMPLICATIONS	REMARKS
1730 to 1854 (UK)	"Tonnage Rule" "Custom House Rule"	$\text{Tonnage} = \dfrac{\text{Length} \times \text{beam} \times \text{Depth of hold}}{96}$	Length – measured along the keel	Seconds per ton per mile (Mr Ackers 1730)	Free length achieved by rounding forefoot raking sternpost Sail area not included	* 'Builders old Measurement' one of many such "tonnage" rules since UK Act of Parliament in 1694 for calculating number of "tuns" (or casks) in merchantmen.
1854 to 1886 (UK)	"Thames Measurement" Yacht Racing Association (YRA) 1881	$\dfrac{(\text{Length}-\text{beam}) \times \text{beam} \times \frac{1}{2}\text{beam}}{94} = \text{Tons Thames}$ $\dfrac{(L+B)^2}{1730} = B$	Length – foreside of stem to aft side of sternpost at deck level. Beam – Maximum beam L = LWL	Seconds per ton per mile NYS (1868) adjustment. Schooners at tonnage. Yawls at 1½ tonnage. Cutters at 2½ tonnage.	Excessive tax on beam produced increasingly narrow hulls – 'plank on edge' – No tax on sail area so also over canvassed.	Thames Rule (Revised 1962) still in use as measure of yacht size.
1887 UK 1883 USA 1890 USA	Dixon Kemp's Rule (YRA 1888) Seawanhaka Rule New York Yacht Club	$Rating = \dfrac{LWL \times Sail\ Area}{6000}$ $Rating\ or\ \text{"Sail Tons"} = \dfrac{L \times SA}{4000}$ $\dfrac{L+\sqrt{SA}}{2} = Racing\ Length$	1. LWL = DWL = L 2. Sail Area – working sail area.	1. Seconds per mile for rating 2. Level by rating Classes:– UK : 5 Raters, One Raters; USA : 30 foot; 40 foot	Long untaxed overhangs Light displacement Small sail area Excessive beam Low freeboards	Rating was roughly equal to tonnage volume. The rules that produced the "skimming dishes"
1896 (UK)	YRA linear rule	$\dfrac{L + B + \frac{3}{4}G + \frac{1}{2}SA}{2}$ = Rating in feet or metres $R = \dfrac{L + 2d + \frac{3}{4}\sqrt{S} - F}{2.37}$	1. L = LWL 2. B = Max Beam 3. G = Skin girth at midship section from WL to WL 4. SA = Sail area	1. Seconds per mile on rating 2. Rating classes	Long overhangs Freeboard reduced to cut down girth measurement Fillets introduced between hull and keel on Bulb keel yachts.	Rule failed in its intention of eliminating the skimming dish (Rule invented by R.E. Froude, son of pioneer of tank testing, William Froude)
1906 (UK) →	First IYRU Rule Current Rule	Rating (in metres) $= L = \dfrac{B + \frac{2}{3}G + 3d + \frac{1}{3}\sqrt{S} - F}{2}$ $R = \dfrac{L + 2d + \frac{3}{4}\sqrt{S} - F}{2.37}$	1. L measured between girths 2. F = Freeboard calculation. 3. O = Girth differences	–ditto–	Skimming dishes eliminated Freeboards raised Scow form discouraged	First International Rule excluded USA Created great Metre (6, 8, 12 etc.) Classes. United States joined IYRU in 1921
1909 USA	Herreshoff's Universal Rule	$R = 0.18L \times \dfrac{\sqrt{S}}{\sqrt[3]{DISP}}$	1. L measured parallel to centre line at ½Bmax. 2. Disp from designer	1. Seconds per mile 2. One-design classes.	Scow hull form penalised	Used for J Class and slightly modified for 1926 Fastnet.
1912	Boat Racing Association	$R = \dfrac{1}{3}\dfrac{\sqrt{SA}}{\sqrt[3]{D}} + .25L + .25\sqrt{SA}$	1. L measured parallel to centreline 2. Displacement from designer 3. SA as IYRU	1. Time on time or 2. Time on distance		BRA Rule combines Seawanhaka and Universal Rules NB "The worst measurement rule ever produced"

86

OFFSHORE RACING

DATES	RATING RULE	FORMULA	MEASUREMENT	TIME ALLOWANCE	DESIGN IMPLICATIONS	REMARKS
1866 to 1928	Transatlantic Races Sailed Level	None	None	None		Most yachts of the same size, type and rig. Major disparity occurred in Kaiser's Cup in 1905 'Fleur de Lys' LWL 87 feet 'Atlantic' 135 feet LWL.
1906 to 1910	First Bermuda Races	Simple length Measurement	-	Length reduced to minutes per foot for the entire course	Not applicable	All cruising yachts of similar type
1923 to 1926	Bermuda Races	LOA only		Sixty Seconds per foot of LOA for the course of 660 NM	Value of short ends so that LWL and LOA are nearly equal	Tended to favour smaller yachts. First yacht built for min LOA
1925	RORC	Rating = $\dfrac{L + \sqrt{S} - F}{5} + 0.1\dfrac{L\sqrt{S}}{\sqrt[3]{D}}$	1. L measured parallel to centreline. 2. S = 1/7RU sail area. 3. F = Freeboard to top of rail. 4. Displacement from design	Time on time or Time on distance	-	Cruising canvas only. Only use of displacement by RORC.
1926 1928 1932	RORC Bermuda	$R = \dfrac{.2L \times \sqrt{S}}{\sqrt{BD}}$	1. L = Between perpendiculars with freeboard factor. 2. Depth from top of beams	-ditto-	-	US used 4% LWL plane for L and introduced rig allowances.
1931 to 1970	RORC	$R = 0.15\dfrac{L\sqrt{S}}{\sqrt{BD}} + 0.2(L + \sqrt{S})$	1. L - Between girth stations. 2. Draught Limits 3. Sheer limits 4. Rig Allowances 5. Scantling component	Time correction factor = $\sqrt{\dfrac{Rating + 2.06}{10}}$	Vulnerability to light displacement/high freeboard reduced by 19.	Rule modified frequently over years. Included stability alls, propellor allowance.
1934 to 1970	CCA	$R =$ .95 $\left(\dfrac{L}{4} \pm \text{Draft} \pm \text{Dis} \pm \text{SA} - \text{Freeboard} \pm \text{Iron Keel}\right)$ x Ballast Ratio x Propellor factor	1. L measured on plane 4% LWL above waterline. 2. Draft and displacement from designer	Nayru time allowance tables - ie time on distance.	Beamy boats favoured shallow draft bonus	CCA rule took 'base' dimensions for ideal yacht against 'L' and then awarded penalties or bonuses for disparities. 'Base' values amended to avoid abuses and to keep abreast of developments
1970 to 1973	International Offshore Rule Mark II IOR Mark III (to 1976)	Rating = $\left(.13\dfrac{L \times \sqrt{S}}{\sqrt{B} \times D} + .25L + .2\sqrt{S} + DC + FC\right)$ x EPF x CGF	1. L measured over girth stations. 2. Immersed depth only. 3. Draft correction. 4. Freeboard correction. 5. Engine & propellor factor. 6. Centre of gravity factor.	Time on time or time on distance. scale. Fixed rating classes. Performance factor system.	See Chapter Six	Features of both RORC and CCA Rules combined. Comprehensive and flexible measurement system subject to rapid review to thwart rule-cheating.

which reflected the experience of the highly competitive nineteenth-century inshore scene. Since, as we saw in chapter 1, rule-cheaters tend not just to change the rules but also to improve them, the origins of the superb cruiser-racers of the present day lie with the 'plank on edge' and 'skimming dish' freaks of the Victorian era.

In the days of yachting innocence, passage races were usually raced level and the vagaries of sea, wind and tide completely obscured what were then comparatively minor differences in size and rig. Yachting was a casual affair of private races and wagers without the serious intent and strict organisation it was later to achieve. When racing in sheltered waters called for some form of handicapping resort was made to the 'tonnage rule'. This was based on an Act of Parliament of 1694 which stipulated a means by which it was possible to estimate the number of 'tuns' that could be accommodated in a merchant ship. (A 'tun' was 252 gallons of wine.) The method of calculation in the United Kingdom was known as the 'builders' old measurement' (BOM) and I have given the formula in the Table (p 86). That yachts had neither holds nor 'tonnage' decks was a mere technicality because at the time yachts were essentially small ships with specially fitted interiors. Having determined the 'tonnage' of a yacht under BOM, it was given a time-allowance based on a scale devised by a calculating gentleman called Mr Ackers and used since about 1730. In the consternation created by the *America*'s victory in 1851 British yachtsmen and builders awoke to the possibilities of beating the BOM rule. The rule itself taxed keel length but not waterline length so stern posts were given an enormous rake and the hitherto straight stems and sharp forefoots were rapidly replaced by a cut-away profile and a short keel. The BOM rule also taxed beam but neither draft nor sail-area were taken into account. It was therefore a comparatively easy development to reduce beam to the minimum and increase draft and ballast to attain the stability to support a massive sail-area. These new 'rule-cheaters' began to dominate the racing field and yachting's age of innocence – if it ever existed – was gone.

The reaction came in 1854 when the Royal London and the Royal Mersey changed the basis upon which length was measured under the tonnage rule to the point where the newer designs were heavily handicapped against the old 'straight stemmers'. This was an equally unsatisfactory development and the Royal Thames stepped in with its famous rule which, as we have seen in chapter 2, is still in use today – but not for rating purposes outside the 'Tall Ships' Races. The weakness here was again the excessive tax on beam although this was done with the best intentions. It was appreciated at the time that draft should be taxed. Draft however is not easy to measure and as it usually approximated half the beam then '$\frac{1}{2}B$' was used in the formula instead. Sail-area again was not taxed and length was measured from stem to stern post. This let in the sharp designers who arranged for the stern post to come well inside the waterline. *Jullanar*, a notorious 'rule-cheater' of the day – her designer, incidentally, was an agricultural implement maker – had her stern post 16 ft inside the after-end of her waterline – a not inconsiderable gain on a 100 ft waterline. She remained true too to the narrow beam, deep draft tradition but had a cut-away forefoot. She was also heavily canvassed. All these characteristics were encouraged by the Thames Rule.

Once again there was reaction. A body of yachtsmen set themselves up as the 'Yachting Racing Association' with the avowed intention of controlling the designers and eliminating the 'rule-cheaters'. Their first move was to amend the Thames Rule to remove the advantages of kinked rudder posts and crank-shaped stern posts. Eventually they came to realise that the length measurement was at fault and they amended this aspect of the rule to require length to be measured along the waterline rather than along the deck and science had at last begun to take a hand. But the revised rule – Appendix C – still had many of the failings of the older Thames rule and unhealthy, over-canvassed, over-ballasted planks-on-edge still continued to proliferate. The tradition of the heavy-displacement, narrow-beamed and over-canvassed British yacht was being established.

Across the Atlantic during the same period, the Americans had replaced the 'Custom House Rule' which was the equivalent of the British BOM with a rule based on displacement. This overlooked that length not weight or sheer size is the criterion of speed in yachts. It resulted in the development of yachts of comparatively light displacement and with the displacement well spread over a long waterline. (*America*, with a displacement/length ratio of 200, is indicative of this trend which itself was in keeping with the older American work-boat tradition of shallow draft and centreboards.) In 1856 a new rule was introduced which classified yachts on a basis of their sail-area but was later abandoned in favour of a return to a variation of the Custom House Rule. It was however in force long enough to encourage moderate sail-areas above large hulls where shallow draft tended to limit the range of stability.

The revised American Custom House Rule was in effect a measure of the internal volume of a yacht but it was measured in such a way that it tended to discourage both draft and freeboard. In consequence the ability to carry adequate sail became increasingly dependent upon wide beam for its stability. Capsizes, particularly at moorings, became frequent and the wide low freeboard hull was as unhealthy a development in American waters as was the British plank-on-edge with 'a lead mine in her keel'. There then occurred on both sides of the Atlantic a complete change in the approach to rating, inspired no doubt by the steady increase in understanding of the scientific aspects of yacht design. First, in the United States, the Seawanhaka Yacht Club of New York brought in the 'Seawanhaka Rule' which completely abondoned the 'tonnage' concept and produced a linear measure in feet. The Rule as it finally emerged was essentially simple: Length plus the square root of sail-area divided by two. Four years later the Dixon Kemp proposals for a rule based on length and sail-area alone was adopted by the YRA in the United Kingdom. Dixon Kemp was one of the great pioneers of scientific yacht design and it was he in his books on yacht design and yacht architecture who was first responsible for offering the lay yachtsmen an insight into the technicalities of the sport. His proposal was also simple: LWL times Sail-area divided by 6,000 – giving a numerical rating roughly equal to the tonnage volume. In short, a rating in terms which yachtsmen of the day could readily appreciate. (There is incidentally no evidence to suggest that there was any transatlantic poaching of the linear/sail-area idea. It is much more likely that informed opinion on both sides of the Atlantic saw this particular device as a solution to trends and tendencies in design they were anxious to arrest.) Unfortunately it resulted in the development of the 'skimming dish' – a light beamy hull with little depth and freeboard and with long flat overhangs so the immersed length nearly doubled when the yacht heeled. Keels were of the short fin and bulb type. Nonetheless, the length/sail area idea is a simple and practical method of handicapping yachts of similar size and type when its design implications are not significant. The Seawanhaka Rule, for example, was, to my personal knowledge, still in use in Florida in 1965.

In an attempt to eliminate the 'skimming dish' the United Kingdom adopted R. E. Froude's 'Linear Rule' which introduced a skin girth factor with the intention of encouraging fuller hulls. Beam also became a factor again. The attempt was however unsuccessful because designers merely fitted fillets between the fin keel and the hull body and reduced the girth measurement. They then went on cheerfully with low freeboard and long flat ends. Froude's Rule was revised in 1901 and when the European nations got together in 1906 and founded the International Yacht Racing Union (IYRU), it formed the basis of the first IYRU rating rule:

$$R = \frac{L+B+\frac{1}{2}G+3d+\frac{1}{3}\sqrt{S}-F}{2}$$

In this rule, d was the girth difference between a chain drawn tight around the hull and one which followed the skin. This served to penalise the fin keel and also to encourage greater displacement. L was measured between girths round the ends and F was a freeboard factor. R was in metres – the origin in fact of the rule which produced the metre boats – the 6m, 8m and 12m which between the wars made up the bulk of the inshore racing classes. The current IYRU rule which still covers the 12m yachts competing in the America's Cup contest is:

$$R = \frac{L+2d+\sqrt{S}-F}{2\cdot37}$$

The United States, which did not join the IYRU until 1921, adopted a different solution to the 'skimming dish' problem. For our purpose it is a significant one:

$$R = \frac{0\cdot18L\times\sqrt{S}}{\sqrt[3]{\text{Displacement}}}$$

This was the Universal Rule and it was devised after considerable research by Nathanael G. Herreshoff, an all-time great among American designers. (He also devised the scantling rule which was mentioned in the previous chapter.) The Universal Rule was introduced in 1909. Readers of this book will have met it somewhere before! It was widely used in the United States for numerous inshore classes, including some one-designs until the Americans agreed to use the IYRU rule for international racing in 1921. Thereafter the Universal Rule covered only the very largest yachts – the immortal 'J' class of the 1930s, about 86 ft on the waterline, which included yachts like *Britannia*, *Shamrock*, *Rainbow* and *Endeavour*. The other Universal class which attained prominence in the United States, the 'M' class (54 ft LWL) falling roughly between the 12 m IYRU (45 ft LWL) boat and the Js, was never introduced into European waters.

But though the IYRU rule is still extant for the America's Cup at least, the Universal Rule faded out with the 'Js' at the end of the 1930s. Its basic principle has, however, been preserved. In 1912, a group of dissident yachtsmen (a recurring phenomenon on the sailing scene) wishing to race yachts not covered by the IYRU rule formed the 'Boat Racing Association' and invited Major Malden Heckstall-Smith – a foremost authority of the day and himself another 'all time great', this time British – to devise a rule which would permit racing between a variety of types. He produced a blend of the main elements of the Universal and the Seawanhaka Rules:

$$R = \frac{1}{3}\frac{L\times\sqrt{S}}{\sqrt[3]{\text{Disp}}} + 0\cdot25L + 0\cdot24\sqrt{S}$$

The yachting pundits of the day, eager as ever to pour scorn on inventive upstarts, described the new Rule as 'the worst measurement rule ever produced' and one which 'measured length and sail area to death'. Although the BRA itself foundered, the rule worked well and demonstrated its ability to produce close corrected times among a varied range of yachts. It did so well, in fact, that fifty-six years later a consortium of the world's leading designers and rating authorities selected a formula very like it as the basis of the world's first International Offshore Rule. So much, then, for pundits. But there is rather more to it than that.

Offshore racing started like inshore racing with a few private races across the Atlantic where yachts, mostly of a size, raced level. In 1906 the first race to Bermuda from Marblehead, Mass, was organised by the editor of *The Rudder*, Thomas Fleming Day, the father of modern ocean-racing. As the race attracted a variety of sizes of yacht, he devised a simple handicap system. Based on length alone it arrived at so many minutes per foot of length for the entire course. It worked well enough although it was essentially a time-allowance device for yachts of a similar type and did not aim at controlling the type of yacht which might be built specifically for the Bermuda Race. This did not happen until 1926 and in the meantime the Bermuda Race had undergone a number of vicissitudes. In 1907 it became a race for what Tom Day himself called 'stinkboats' as well as sailing craft, and after the race of 1910 it died out altogether until another prominent yachting journalist, Herbert L. Stone, editor of *Yachting*, persuaded a group of fellow-members of the Cruising Club of America to revive the event in 1923, the CCA itself finally taking over management of the race in 1926. The rating system used for the 1923 Bermuda followed the Day system and was based on overall-length alone. There was no allowance for rig and for time allowance a flat figure of 60 min/ft of length for the course of 660 nautical miles was used. This was reduced in 1924 to 45 min/ft and in 1926 a rig allowance was also introduced. The same year saw the first entry built with the time-allowance system in view – to secure a favourable 'rating' under the overall length measurement – *Dragoon*. She had a long waterline and short ends and a massive sail-area. She did not, as it happens, win the race (she was second), but the simple time-allowance system was sufficiently effective to bring in the first four boats within four hours of corrected time after about five days. But once again the age of innocence was just about over and the CCA in 1928 'borrowed' the Royal Ocean Racing Club's formula for the Bermuda Race of that year.

For the first Fastnet in 1925 the Ocean Racing Club – the Royal had still to be earned – had adopted a variation of the Boat Racing Association rule which as we saw earlier had been devised by Malden Heckstall-Smith to enable different types to race against each other, and was a combination of the American Universal Rule and the Seawanhaka Rule. I have given details in Fig 15 of the formula which was used only for the one race and it is of interest because it used for the only time in RORC history the actual value of displacement. The following year the RORC adopted the square root of the beam × the internal depth as being easier and cheaper to measure and verify. (This factor has appeared in its rules ever since.) Other features of the first rule that are of interest are that the rule stipulated that only cruising canvas could be used – an interdiction which clearly could not last – and provided a bonus for high freeboard. The 1926 Rule – and that adopted by the CCA – was our old friend:

$$\text{Rating in feet} = 0.2 \left(\frac{L \times \sqrt{S}}{\sqrt{BD}} \right).$$

L was measured between perpendiculars plus one-quarter of the difference between this

LBP and the LOA minus the height of the bulwarks amidships from covering board to the top of the rail. (At this time bulwarks were regarded as essential in seagoing craft.) The other measurement of historical interest is that of D – depth – which was the depth measured from the top of the beams at the side amidships to the top of the floors. After 1926 the method of measuring length was altered to bring in a system of length between fore and aft girth stations with the girths being determined by the beam of the yacht. This feature has also been retained ever since. In 1931, however, the 1926 formula was amended and the basic RORC formula became what it remained until 1970 when it was subsumed in the International Offshore Rule. This is:

$$\text{Rating in feet} = 0.15\frac{L\sqrt{S}}{\sqrt{BD}} + 0.2\,(L+\sqrt{S}).$$

What did change over the years was the manner in which the various measurements were made. We shall be looking into the more important of these but the major impact of the RORC rule on offshore yacht design on this side of the Atlantic was not so much that of the restrictions it imposed but of the freedom it allowed. The years of the 1930s saw a slow transformation of the offshore yacht from the traditional cruiser which raced – *Jolie Brise*, designed *c*. 1900, won the Fastnet in 1929 and 1930 – to the racing yacht which was capable of going to sea. The old trusted and tried features of heavy displacement, long keel, deep forefoot – 'to get a grip on the sea when hove to' – and the gaff rig were slowly being replaced by the lighter build and displacement short, cut away keels and Bermudian masts and rig of the inshore classes, notably of the IYRU classes. *Dorade*, who as we saw in chapter 1 was the first design dedicated to ocean-racing to arrive on the British scene, was essentially an IYRU design, only her draft going outside the limits of that rule. The point here is that the new RORC rule, despite the preoccupation of its creators with safety at sea, never attempted to freeze offshore yacht design into the traditional 'trustworthy' mould. Indeed, in some respects, it ushered in a new era of what we would nowadays call 'permissiveness' in design, particularly on the question of masts and rig. The IYRU, for example, restricted the height of the mast and that of the foretriangle to three-quarters of the mast. This precluded mast-head rig. Furthermore, the IYRU restricted the amount of overlap possible in the biggest headsail. The RORC Rule however imposed no such restrictions. It was therefore in the offshore fleet in the late 1930s that the most rapid evolution of modern sail plans and rigging occurred. The testing ground was no longer the sheltered waters of the Solent but the rigours of the Fastnet gale and the Channel chop. And the new ideas stood up to the test and the offshore yacht became the source of its own development. It was at this point, perhaps, that obsolescence and eventual extinction set in for the bigger inshore-racing classes and another race of dinosaurs began to die off. 'Adapt or die' applies to yachts as well as mammoths.

One could argue too that the freedom which the RORC Rule gave to designers was in

Opposite, top: the shape of yachts to come? The Australian Admiral's Cup contender Gingko, *designed by Bob Miller. Notice how far forward the mast is and how close to the deck the boom comes.* Bottom: Gingko *exposed. The maximum beam is well forward; she is a latter-day 'cod's head and mackerel tail' – deep full bow sections with a finely tapering stern. There is a slight 'bustle' and the skin is carried aft of the transom to form 'planing boards'.*

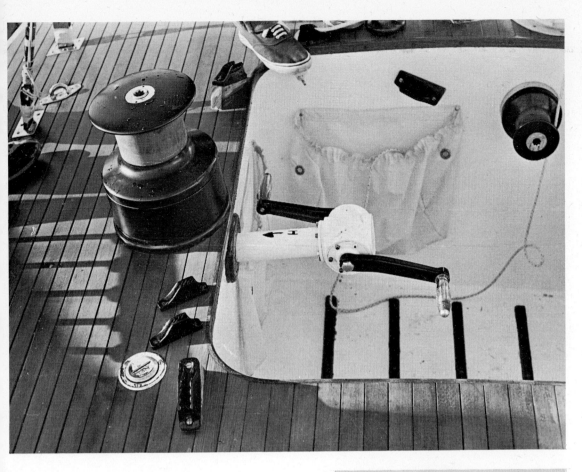

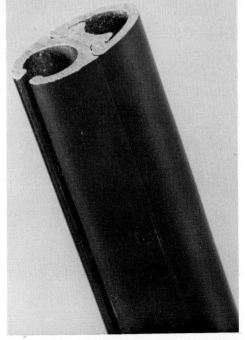

Left: Gingko *again, showing the stern in more detail. The rudder is transom-hung with only a small skeg, but the aspect ratio is typical of modern thinking.*

Above: *coffee-grinder crank handles and separate winch drums constitute a modern crew position known as 'ant-hill'. This is also* Gingko.

Right: Sail Keda. *This device improves the aerodynamic efficiency of the leading edge of the foresail by eliminating many of the excrescences which cause turbulent flow or create parasite drag. Further development of ideas such as this may one day bring us to the wing sail, where the mast itself becomes an integral part of the mainsail.*

Equation. *This is a Britton-Chance-designed light displacement ketch which has what is in effect a double sloop rig. It combines the advantage of the single-masted rig on the wind with those of the ketch – including the rating advantage – off it. Notice the large gap between the main and the mizzen masts to avoid downwash effects.*

96

part responsible for the snub-bowed light-displacement yacht of the early post-war years. The original rule had specified that the scantlings of yachts entering for any of the Club's ocean-races 'must be of a strength equivalent to that required by Lloyd's for cruising yachts'. As we have seen in chapter 4 this would have made yachts of heavy construction virtually *de rigeur*. In practice, too, it soon became apparent that the scantling condition was unworkable unless the Club was prepared to disqualify about three-quarters of the current fleet. In 1935 therefore the Club replaced the scantling prohibition with a scheme of scantling allowances based upon the weight of a square foot of the yacht's topsides and deck. This was converted into an allowance which was subtracted from the rating. This left the way clear for designers to introduce strong light methods of construction and clear too for the great post-war 'New Look' in the shape – literally – of *Myth of Malham*.

As we have mentioned earlier, the RORC had from the earliest days of ocean racing under its jurisdiction insisted that the only measurements that should be used in determining a yacht's rating should be those obtainable from a yacht in full commission and afloat. This precluded certificates from designers for factors like displacement which were difficult to measure. For this reason, the RORC dropped the displacement term from the old Universal rule formula and substituted the square root of beam × depth. Until 1949, depth was measured from the deck beams to the floors. This meant that depth was in fact the sum of free-board and immersed depth. Thus a light displacement hull with a high freeboard would have the same depth measurement as a heavy displacement yacht with a low freeboard. Depth measurement was thus independent of the speed-reducing factor, displacement, it was intended to measure. This was the hole in the early RORC Rule through which *Myth of Malham* sailed with the added advantage that her high freeboard and short snubbed ends gave under the length measurements of the rule. But she was more than just a rule-beater – she was in-herently a very fast yacht and she continued to win even after the rule had been changed to remove a great deal of her original advantage. As we have seen, she was the first of a new type of ocean-racing yacht: light construction, light displacement, straight sheerline, snubbed ends. Her rig too – mast almost amidships, high aspect ratio sail plan with large foretriangle and small mainsail – was an innovation, but one which in no way exploited anything but the inherent freedom of the rule. In terms of yacht architecture she was a daring experiment for which at the time there was no precedent. But her inspiration stemmed not so much from an advance in yacht technology as from the desire to exploit the vagaries of the current rating rule. In this sense she was a 'product' of the RORC Rule, however much some of the pundits of the day would have preferred to disown her.

The RORC Rule was revised in 1949 as a 'temporary measure' not to penalise the new generation of light displacement yachts built on the *Myth of Malham* example, but more to provide a fairer assessment of their speed potential compared with what were then more normal types. These amendments were only partly successful and the rule underwent a major review and revision in the period 1954–7. That review confirmed the validity of the basic formula of the rule. The method of measuring length was revised to ensure that it was largely unaffected by freeboard itself but that lower floatation and fullness in the overhangs – condi-tions which would imply an increase in LWL with heel – was appropriately taxed. The 1957 amendment was the last before the RORC Rule was amalgamated – or, if you prefer it, con-glomerated – into the International Offshore Rule which we shall be considering in detail in the next chapter. In its 45-year history it had achieved its purpose brilliantly. It had enabled yachts of widely different types and size to race against each other not just in 'open waters' but in the major inshore events as well where it was increasingly being adopted by regatta authorities throughout the world. Many yachts which never intended to race offshore nonetheless were measured and had rating certificates from the RORC. But the administration of the rule remained essentially a private affair controlled by the Club's Committees in London despite the fact that the writ of the RORC Rule covered virtually the whole of the civilised sailing world outside the North American continent. (Even Iron Curtain countries observed its tenets.) The rule too had achieved its secondary purpose of encouraging the design of fast, safe, offshore yachts. Paradoxically, its only serious weakness – the early depth factor – was in the longer term to prove to be one of its greatest blessings. If the loophole through which *Myth of Malham* sailed had not existed or had the rule itself been less permissive of innovation, the light displacement 'revolution' would at least have been postponed. As it was the *Myth*'s exploitation of the early rule made possible the small highly buoyant offshore yacht and thousands of people have had their lives enriched because of it.

In its final form the RORC Rule was as follows:

$$\text{Measured rating} = 0 \cdot 15 \frac{L\sqrt{S}}{\sqrt{BD}} + 0 \cdot 2\,(L+S)$$

Rating = Measured rating ± Stability allowance − Propeller allowance + Draft Penalty.

The Cruising Club of America used the RORC Rule for the Bermuda Race for the years up to 1934 but modified the method of measuring L to that of the waterline plane 4 per cent of LWL above the water. This procedure was opposed not just in practice but also in principle to the RORC method of L measurement which employed girth stations. The RORC had always set its face against measuring LWL afloat because of the difficulties involved and despite occasional controversy has maintained that position to the present day. The Americans however maintained – as Alf Loomis puts it – '. . . this horizontal plane (i.e. the 4 per cent LWL plane) comes very close to the sailing line of a yacht when heeled. After all it is the length on which a boat sails rather than her overall length that governs her speed'. They were prepared to measure LWL when afloat and they re-issued their declaration of independence from the British yoke in 1934 when they introduced their own rule – the CCA Rule – which remained in force until the IOR merger of 1970.

The CCA Rule was fundamentally different in concept from the RORC Rule despite the fact that the latter had impeccable Transatlantic antecedents. The reasons for this lie in part in the differing types of cruising yacht which had evolved on either side of the Atlantic by the early 1930s. In British waters the faster type of cruiser had still to evolve from the interbreeding of the traditional inshore racing type with the heavy, slow workboat type of cruiser. In American waters, this evolution had already largely taken place and though refinement was necessary the cruisers that existed in the early 1930s were highly suited to offshore racing. Evidence of this difference in the stage of evolution is only too apparent from the ease with which American yachts like *Nina* and *Dorade* crossed the Atlantic and cleaned up the Fastnet. Thus whereas the British needed a Rule which encouraged innovation the Americans could be content to measure and rate their yachts against what they regarded as the desirable norm. Writing at the time, Alf Loomis puts it like this:

In principle this Rule (i.e. CCA) was built around a normal boat of a type accepted as desirable for ocean racing and cruising . . .

Taking the 4 per cent waterline plane as the basis of length measurement, the ends were controlled to prevent excessive overhang forward and aft; a normal (*sic*) ratio of beam to length was worked out; a desirable displacement in the same manner, and mast heights were also regulated. Yachts varying from the normal in any of the various factors of the rule were either penalised for any discrepancy or given a premium for exceeding the requirements. For instance, a boat narrower than the the norm, or with less displacement has the excess (sometimes doubled or trebled) (*sic*) added to her rating, as found by the formula, while one with broader beam or greater displacement has such excess deducted. This results in a wide latitude as to form and sail area, and tends to keep the design of new yachts built to the rule close to the normal.

All of which to my mind smacks in rating terms of the old yacht chandlers' maxim: 'You can have any colour you like provided it's white.' But to be fair to the CCA Rule, it did not postulate an unchanging 'norm' and the base requirement was subject to frequent change as design progressed. And in the ultimate test of the influence of any rating rule upon yacht design – the performance of the boats it inspired – its record is unsurpassed. Boats either owned or designed by Americans dominated the offshore scene on both sides of the Atlantic – and they still do!

The formula for the CCA Rule was:

$$\text{Rating} = 0.95(L \pm \text{Beam} \pm \text{Draft} \pm \text{Disp} \pm \text{Sail area} \pm \text{Freeboard} - \text{Iron keel credit}) \times \text{Ballast ratio} \times \text{Propeller factor}$$

and very conveniently – the inherent simplicity of the rule has been a major factor in its effectiveness – the effect of these individual factors can be summarised as follows:

Factor	Large	Small
Beam	Credit	Penalty
Draft	Penalty	Credit
Displacement	Credit	Penalty
Sail-area	Penalty	Credit
Freeboard	Credit	Penalty
Iron keel	Credit for yachts having an iron keel instead of a lead keel	
Ballast ratio	Penalty	Credit
Propeller Factor	More credit for large propeller, less for small	

In practice the CCA Rule produced hulls of fairly ample length/displacement ratios and tended to discourage the light displacement tendencies apparent in British waters. Beam/length ratios were also generous, and as there was no girth station to take into account, fairly full powerful end sections were usual as were tucked up counters. To accommodate ample displacement and equally ample beam, without excessive wetted surface, the garboard turn tended to be filled in and the bilge-line slackened. Sail-area to displacement tended to be more generous with the CCA than with the RORC Rule and British yachts racing in the Bermuda could usually add 10 per cent to the sail-area optimum for RORC. On the other hand, the CCA severely taxed aspect ratio in both mainsails and fore-triangles – in favour of a low value.

All this experience of the problems of rating, measuring and time allowance (an aspect we shall examine in detail in the next chapter), different though it was in detailed practice and principle on different sides of the Atlantic, was nonetheless part of the essential adolescence of offshore racing as a sport. A period, in fact, that it would have been difficult to avoid, even if, as some pundits had hoped, the Americans had retained the RORC Rule in 1934. In fact, though it is fashionable to refer to the so-called 'missed opportunity' and to hint that thereby thirty-six years were wasted, there was in 1934 no reason at all why the Americans should have accepted a British rule or vice versa. Ocean-racing on both sides of the Atlantic was still in an uncertain infancy – there were only twenty-nine starters in the 1934 Bermuda, all American, and only six in the 1933 Fastnet, three British and three American. A period of intense struggles for simple survival as a national sport – the RORC at that time was also short of members – is hardly conducive to international co-operation. On both sides of the Atlantic there was still a long way to go both in yacht design and development and in cultivating the habit of working with friendly rivals. For the one, another thirty years of experience was required and for the other six years of war was to provide a foundation which made the post-war scene utterly remote from the earlier epoch. The time was not wasted and Douglas Phillips Birt, in his superb official history of the RORC *British Ocean Racing*, sums up the situation thus:

> For the mixed-type cruiser-racer fleets racing under handicap . . . separate rules are best able to cater for national tastes in yachts. Design is not stereotyped and much of value is learned when the yachts of two nations meet and race under the ratings and time allowances of the other's rules. Furthermore, a rule once internationalised becomes harder to administer and control.

But nonetheless, ten years later, in 1970, the kissing stopped and the International Offshore Rule was introduced.

6
Ruling the Offshore World

By the mid-1960s the rate of expansion of the offshore racing fleets in all the major yachting countries completely dwarfed that of the inshore fleets of a century earlier, which had hitherto been regarded as the 'Golden Age of Yachting'. In 1951 there were twenty-nine starters in the Fastnet, in 1955 forty-six yachts started of whom six were American and thirteen came from five other foreign countries. The 1961 Fastnet saw ninety-seven cross the starting-line and this had risen to 151 by 1965. The figure for 1973 was 257 and this included no less than sixteen national teams taking part in the Admiral's Cup contest. Other major events like the Onion Patch Trophy – of which the Bermuda Race is the major event just as the Fastnet is the major event of the Admiral's Cup series – and the celebrated Sydney–Hobart Race all experienced the same burgeoning of competitors. But this represented only the *crème de la crème* of the offshore racing world and for every yacht taking part in major international events there were probably a hundred which all over the world, week by week, raced in local events under either the RORC Rule or the CCA Rule. Furthermore, by the late 1960s, something like 5,000 newly built yachts – most of them series produced – were being added annually to the fleets of cruiser-racers which, if the owner wished, could qualify for a rating under the appropriate rule.

The CCA Rule was primarily national but the RORC held sway over virtually the rest of the world. Although there was never the slightest suggestion that the RORC organisation was not both efficient and fair, the RORC remained a comparatively small and exclusive club. 'Taxation without representation' can never survive for long in a community as democratic in principle as that of the offshore yachtsmen, and there is in yachting history evidence too of a remarkable alacrity to set up international bodies to control the sport. Pressure for an international offshore rule with an appropriate and representative controlling body began to build up. There were other pressures as well. The RORC Rule, last revised in 1957, was in need of revision particularly in the light of the growing interest in fixed-rating events like the One Ton Cup. In international team events 'across the rating barrier', whilst the RORC Rule was not unkind to yachts designed for the CCA, the reverse was emphatically not the case. Finally, the designer who almost uniquely had demonstrated an ability to design winners under either rule (or, indeed, any rule) – Olin Stephens, Jr – declared to the IYRU that in his view a practicable international offshore rule could be devised.

The task fell to a committee headed by Olin Stephens himself and comprising Dick Carter, another American designer with an outstanding record of winners under the RORC Rule, the two top RORC measurers – both British – Major Robin Glover and the late Brigadier L. R. E. Fayle – probably the foremost authority in the world on rules and ratings – and two European designers of distinction in the offshore field, Ricus van de Stadt of Holland and Gustave Plym of Sweden. They took three years to develop the new Rule and the first version, 'Mark I', which was produced for opinion sampling and subsequent revision appeared in November 1968. The first active version was the International Offshore Rule Mark II and it came into effect from January 1970. Subsequently, the International Technical Committee (ITC), as Olin Stephens's committee became known, recommended further adjustments to the Offshore Rating Council (ORC) – now the controlling body of the sport – and these were introduced at the discretion of the national authorities between April 1972 and 1 January 1973. The IOR Mark III should now remain in force until 1 January 1976 except for such changes as 'may be required to meet circumstances at present unforeseen'. It is by previous standards a massive document covering about 40 quarto pages and paragraph 201 states categorically: 'It is desirable that the owner should be familiar with all parts of the measurement rule.'

In style and complexity the IOR Mark III is truly a 'space age' comparater. But its object hardly needs repeating here because it was that of many previous rules: the rating of yachts of varying size, shape and build so that they can race against each other equitably and, second, to encourage the design of fast, seaworthy yachts without undesirable features. That no rule made by men, even yachtsmen, can cover all circumstances is acknowledged by the Rule's originators. The Offshore Rating Council reserves the right to modify the rule 'from time to time as research or new development may show this to be necessary'. Furthermore, designers introducing 'questionable details or forms' are invited to consult the Council beforehand although the Council has made it clear that their intention is not to discourage development tending to increase the speed of yachts but 'to minimise the incorporation of features tending by unusual methods to reduce the rating'. The Rule, as we have seen, has already been amended once in its brief history and though the Council has indicated its intention that the Rule should be stable, the risks of continuous and repeated amendment seem considerable.

In this chapter I cannot hope to explain in detail how the IOR Mark III is intended to work. I shall therefore content myself by outlining the way in which the Rule assesses the speed potential of a yacht and as far as is possible so early in the life of the Rule, estimate its likely effect upon yacht design. Let us begin then with the basic formula:

$$\text{Measured rating, } MR = \frac{0 \cdot 13 L \sqrt{S}}{\sqrt{B \times D}} + 0 \cdot 25L + 0 \cdot 20 \sqrt{S} + DC + FC$$

where Rating, $R = $ MR $\times$ EPF $\times$ CGF and $L = $ length, $B = $ beam,
$D = $ depth, DC is draft correction, FC is freeboard correction,
EPF is Engine and Propeller Factor, CGF is Centre of Gravity Factor

The basic formula is very simple and readers will already have recognised that it is no more than a development of the RORC formula which was itself a derivative of the BRA Rule and all are based on the ratio of sail-area (power) to displacement (weight) which we met in chapter 3. The IOR uses the same mathematical variables but its constants are altered slightly to permit the inclusion of the new term DC (Draft Correction) and FC (Freeboard Correction) whilst still ensuring that the final outcome in linear units will be not far removed from the yacht's actual length. Linear sail dimensions are measured to one place of decimals (two places for metric units) and all other measurements to two places of decimals (three places metric) but sail-area is taken to one place (two places metric). Numerical factors are calculated to four decimal places. The calculations – a task for the computer – are usually taken to three places of decimals in feet, four in metres, but the final rating is given to one place of decimals in feet, two in metres. This final rounding up of the figure is intended to eliminate experimental error and differences between yachts which may not truly be valid. The range of rating under the IOR is from 16·0 ft IOR to 70·0 ft IOR and there is therefore a total of 541 possible ratings. Eventually it is hoped that, as is already happening with the 'Ton' boats, the number of ratings will be steadily reduced to certain fixed values just as the old Metre-IYRU Rule produced the 6 m, 8 m and 12 m yachts. So far fixed ratings have been approved for the following:

	Rating	
Quarter Ton	5·50 m	(18·0 ft)
Half Ton	6·60 m	(21·6 ft)
Three-Quarter Ton	24·5 ft	(7·5 m)
One Ton	27·5 ft	(8·38 m)
Two Ton	33 ft	(10·10 m)
Canada's Cup	32 ft	(9·76 m)*

* The value shown first – feet or metres – indicates the place of origin of the event.

and two other fixed level classes are likely to be introduced in the near future – 37 ft (11·30 m), 41 ft (12·50 m) and 45 ft (13·75 m) to cover the increasing popularity of America's Cup-style 'match' racing in the United States.

One other point worth noting before we leave the main formula and examine its constituents and how they are measured is that in the denominator of the first term the square root of beam × depth is spelled out '$B \times D$'. This is an important convention used throughout the rule which ignores the usual algebraic convention which in the case of this term in the earlier RORC Rule would have been written 'BD'. In the IOR Rule BD would not mean $B \times D$ but 'Boom Depth Main' – a single value. Be warned therefore of the need under the IOR to check on the definition of every term in the glossary, a copy of which is at Appendix C.

The main factors of the rule are L, S, B, D, DC and FC from which the measured rating is calculated and EPF and CGF which qualify MR into final rating.

L, which is rated length, is the key to the whole rating rule representing as it does the latest attempt to measure the effective sailing length of a given hull. In the previous chapter we have seen how earlier attempts were responsible for distortions in hull design. Waterline measurement led to the skimming dish, LOA produced vertical stems and cut off counters. Even the later more sophisticated rules led to some abuses – the CCA Rule prompting particularly wide overhangs because the L measurement depended solely on profile factors and the RORC Rule (which employed girths and ignored profiles), prompting ends that were suddenly pinched in at the girth stations. The new IOR has endeavoured to combine the best of both these worlds. The actual length L used in the formula is the length between girth stations minus the forward overhang component (FOC) and minus the aft-overhang component (AOC). The position of the girths – there are two forward and two aft – is related as in the RORC Rule to the maximum beam. The forward girth station, for example, is at the point where the hull girth equals half the beam and so on for the other girths (see diagram at Appendix C). LBG is the distance between the forward and after girth stations which is a reasonably straightforward measurement. The real difficulties arise over the forward overhang component (FOC) and the aft-overhang component (AOC) which are applied as adjustments to LBG to give first LBGC (length between girth stations corrected) and, finally, L itself.

The size of these components and whether they are positive or negative depends upon the geometric shape of the ends. Bow shapes are determined by design criteria – indeed perhaps by the demands of the sea itself – and do not vary greatly. Freeboard is taken into account favourably in determining FOC and the RORC-Rule-inspired trick of pinching in the lines at the girth stations has been prevented by taking into account the beams on the deck forward and the rate of change of beam between the two adjoining girth stations. This may sound highly complicated – though a glance at the following formula (para 330 of the rule) will, I think, indicate the extent to which I have sought to simplify the complicated arithmetic involved.

$$\text{FOC} = \text{GSDF}\,\frac{FF - 0{\cdot}3B \times 0{\cdot}15BF}{0{\cdot}125B + \text{FSFD} - 0{\cdot}\overline{1}5\text{FSBD}}$$

In fact the calculation of FOC is not so much of a mathematical confidence trick as laymen might believe. Its object is to fix the forward end of L which must lie somewhere between the end of the waterline – something of a movable feast as we have seen – and the very end of the yacht. The function of the complicated arithmetic is to determine the distance from the forward girth station to a point where a theoretical line cuts the waterline extended and the theoretical line itself is determined by the shape of the bow. Already an IOR-type bow has emerged and it looks like the diagram immediately below – straight waterlines, V-sections and a straight stem.

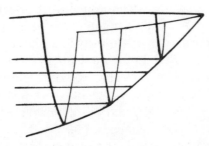

FIG 16   *The shape of the* IOR *Mark* III *bow.*

The measurement of bow shapes is reasonably straightforward and logical. Not so the shape of the sterns – that is the AOC – because of the infinite variety of shapes to rear ends! The principle here is the same as for bows – girth stations, freeboards and deck beams aft are all taken into account and a further ingredient is added in the shape of a 'vertical height aft' and a 'vertical inner height aft' which determines the profile of the stern in a manner not called for in the measurement of bows. Bustles and skegs are accounted for by another measurement called 'Buttock Heights' which, as their name implies, seek to define the shape of the section of the stern. There is also a factor called 'Y' which is defined as the 'normal limit of length aft, special' and this applies to cut-off sterns. As Brigadier Fayle himself put it when writing of the Mark II Rule: 'The after end of L in fact presents the largest stumbling block to the rule-makers.'

The truth of this was borne out in the amendments to the rule which constituted IOR Mark III when the AOC formula was considerably revised. The object of the revision was to sway the measurement more to favour wide, flat sterns – the old GCA sterns – and towards encouraging the extension of normal overhangs by making these less expensive in comparison with the earlier practice of chopping sterns off short. (The expense here means in rating terms only!) But sterns remain devilish difficult and the complexity is summed up in para 332 of the rule at Appendix B.

This extract from IOR Mark III gives an idea of the complexities.

332. Formula for After Overhang Component (AOC).

.1 AOCP is intended to approximate the horizontal distance from AGS to the point at which a line drawn at a distance of 0·018LBGC below the profile intersects the water plane.

.2 AOCG is intended to approximate the horizontal distance from AGS to the point where a line below the sheer line drawn at a distance equal to the half girths of the sections minus 20 per cent of the beam at these sections intersects the water plane.

.3 AOCP and AOCG will normally be satisfactorily determined from the girth stations AGS and AIGS and by the formulae given in the paragraph. If for any reason this procedure appears to give an AOCP or AOCG greatly at variance from the above intentions, the Chief Measurer may at his discretion direct that a yacht shall be measured by girths taken as near as possible to the assumed position of the proper aft end of L.

.4 *Formula for AOCG:*

$$\text{AOCG} - \frac{\text{GSDA (FA} - 0\cdot375\text{B} - 0\cdot5\text{GD} + 0\cdot2\text{BA}}{0\cdot0625\text{B} + \text{FA} - \text{FAI} - 0\cdot2\text{BAI} + 0\cdot2\text{BA}}$$

.5 *Formula for AOCP:*

$$\text{AOCP} = \frac{\text{GSDA (FA} - \text{VHA} - 0\cdot018\text{LBGC)}}{\text{VHAI} - \text{VHA} + \text{FA} - \text{FAI}}$$

Where (FA — VHA — 0·018LBGC) is negative, the factor

$$\frac{\text{GSDA}}{\text{VHAI} - \text{VHA} + \text{FA} - \text{FAI}}$$

shall not be taken as greater than 6·0.

.6 *Formula for AOC:*

$$\text{AOC} = 0\cdot5 \, (\text{AOCP} + \text{AOCG})$$

All of this serves to give substance to the belief that without a computer – or something very much akin to it – designers are hard put to it to sort out the likely effects of minor changes to the lines of the stern. No doubt a standard IOR Mark III stern will emerge in due course but we can expect some distortions to appear before designers are satisfied that the definitive shape has been drawn.

Once *L* has been determined, it is employed in several other formulae connected with the establishment of final rating: freeboard, draft and the speed-generating ability of the yacht's engine. In all of these measurements and calculations it replaces LWL and is in all respects a more reliable measure.

B, beam, is important in determining the position of the girth stations and as a 'speed-reducing factor' it is in the denominator of the main formula which means that a high *B* is a help rather than a hindrance to a low rating. *B* is in fact the easiest factor to measure being – with allowances for raised decks and other features – the maximum beam measured one-sixth of the beam below the sheer line. To prevent designers slipping in a chine at the *B* measurement point specifically to obtain a large *B*, measurers use a spline to fair off the curve of the hull and then subtract the departure from the fair curve from the *B* figure. Thirty years of weeding, mowing and rolling have not entirely been lost on the rule-makers!

The IOR follows the RORC tradition rather than the CCA and does not measure displacement directly – or for that matter wetted surface – but uses the long-established alternative of $\sqrt{B} \times D$ as we saw when looking at the main formula. If, however, *B* is easy to measure, *D*, depth, must of necessity be complex and properly safeguarded. It was through this door marked *D*, remember, that the *Myth of Malham* sailed in 1947 and the weeders, mowers and rollers would never forget an experience like that.

D, rated depth, to give it its full title, is a measure of the amount of the hull in the water. *Myth*'s loophole was that at the time she was designed, *D* included freeboard as well as immersed depth. The RORC rule took care of that anomaly by deleting freeboard from the immersed depth measurement and also introduced the 'Quarter Beam Depth' position whereby the depth amidships was measured not immediately down the centre-line of the hull but at a point one-quarter of the beam offset from it. This device was to ensure that designers did not sharply cut away beam at the waterline. The RORC also measured immersed depth at a forward station and because it gave in its formula determining rated *D* equal weight to both the forward and the midship depths, yachts which were unnecessarily deep forward tended to be produced. The IOR overcomes this by giving more weight – in numerical terms – to the midships depth measurement. It also modifies the RORC method of immersed depth measurement by introducing two additional points to the 'Quarter Beam Depth' measurement at one-eighth and three-eighths *B* from the centre-line. The effect of this is virtually to delineate immersed area of the midship section and effectively to rule out some of the odd shapes which were appearing which, while achieving maximum *D* values, reduced displacement to the minimum. That this latter measure has been introduced only since IOR Mark II became IOR Mark III shows that the tillers of the rating lawn remain as sharp-eyed as ever.

Although the use of $\sqrt{B} \times D$ is a practical method of allowing for displacement without the necessity of actually measuring it, it has the disadvantage that it is inclined to give too low a figure in large yachts compared with the actual value of $\sqrt[3]{\text{Disp}}$. This is unfair to the larger yacht which tends to suffer from the basic structure of the rule anyway as we shall discuss later. To rectify this inequity and to prevent depths from changing sharply with change of trim, there is a last term in the formula for rated *D* that includes rated *L* − *L* + 10 ft/30.

The next major factor in the main part of the formula where, like *L*, it occurs twice, the 'power' or speed-creating factor – sail-area, which for arithmetical tidiness in a linear rule is dealt with as a square root. The principles adopted in sail measurement owes more to the CCA Rule perhaps than to the RORC which dominated in the evolution of hull measurement.

What the rule seeks to do is to measure the geometric area of the sail plan but to apply a weighting factor up or down in accordance with the efficiency of the sail in question. In chapter 3 we saw that headsails are, area for area, more efficient than mainsails. Under the IOR, genoas have their area increased by 30 per cent whereas mainsails have their area reduced by a similar amount for rating purposes. Aspect ratio – also a measure of efficiency in sails, especially to windward – is accounted for in similar way and both the area of the mainsail (RSAM) and the area of the foretriangle (RSAF) have a quantity added to them related to aspect ratio although in this rule, unlike the CCA, both areas are considered separately. This would permit the designer some latitude in positioning his mast to achieve a high aspect ratio main and a lower aspect ratio foretriangle. A mention of aspect ratio reminds me that in chapter 3 we used aspect ratio in its aerodynamic sense – AR = Area/Chord but the IOR uses the simpler ratio we also considered – luff/foot ratio. The AR for the mainsail is therefore P/E and that for the foretriangle I/J. The meaning of these terms is clear from a glance at the diagram at Appendix C (page 40, para 805 *et seq* of the rule), and, to crystallise clarity still further, I will add that the sinister word 'BAD' means nothing more sinister than 'Boom Above Deck'.

Within broad limits the amount of sail a given hull will carry will be determined by design considerations based on the type of sailing she is expected to do most.

Rating requirements will make only marginal adjustments. They will however have more influence upon the choice of rig – whether, for example, the hull should be fitted with the ubiquitous masthead sloop rig, the seven-eighths masthead rig or one of the two-masted rigs if the yacht is big enough for sail-handling difficulties to be a factor. Though the IOR is equipped to deal with the gaff rig, we shall not consider it further. There is no evidence to suggest so far that going even for the best gaff rig that modern design can produce will give a combination of reduced performance and lower rating to make a viable racer – but don't take that for granted! The IOR is a sufficiently free rule for many surprises to be sprung yet upon a stereotyped pattern of offshore design.

At the time that IOR Mark II was introduced, there was a strong design tendency for mainsails to become smaller and foretriangles – and, with them, spinnakers – to become larger. This tendency was not the result of rating rule influence although the old RORC Rule did nothing to discourage it, but the much more telling one of getting the most out of every foot of canvas carried. Spinnakers in particular became infected with a particular virulent form of elephantitis with the introduction of the star-cut which, as we saw in chapter 3, enables spinnakers to be carried far closer to the wind than ever before. The IOR Mark II insisted upon a minimum size of mainsail related to the height of the foretriangle hoist and IOR Mark III introduced two amendments which sought to restrain the apparent design trend. The first of these meant that the rating of the total sail-area will be determined by the sum of 110 per cent of the foretriangle and 85·7 per cent of the mainsail rated areas. The other rule-change limited the size of spinnakers by stipulating in effect that where the size of the spinnaker is greater than the total rated sail-area, the larger figure will count as the total sail-area. IOR Mark III also introduced changes to the aspect ratio element of the formula which is used for calculating the rated sail-area of the foretriangle. Its effect is to reduce slightly the advantages of low aspect foretriangles and spinnakers.

As we have seen from the experience of earlier rating rules, it takes time for changes to be digested and assimilated into actual designs. It is also a difficult matter even with the use of computers to forecast what influence rule changes will have if for no better reason than that the fashion factor plays its part. It is, of course, totally unpredictable for, while yacht designers have little in common with designers of hemlines and such, they do share the artistic desire to be original and to spring the occasional surprise. We shall, however, play the guessing game in the next chapter. For the moment it is perhaps enough to say that under the revised IOR Mark III rules which affect sail-area, the rating effects of increasing the size of spinnakers will on a foot-for-foot basis be the same as that of increasing mainsails. Which then should one go for? Whilst the numerous masthead sloops now extant are unlikely to be affected, the seven-eighths rig and the two-masted rigs, especially the schooner, are likely to benefit against the sloops – in terms of rating that is.

So much for the factor S or $\sqrt{S}$. We have now seen how, in general terms, the IOR Mark III assesses the main components of the basic formula – L, B, D and S. There remain now DC (draft correction), FC (freeboard correction), which directly affect measured rating, and the two other factors EPF (engine and propeller factor) and CGF (centre of gravity factor), which serve to determine actual rating from measured rating.

'Freeboard correction' is the most straightforward of the four factors. The principle is that there is a fixed 'base' freeboard which depends upon the L measurement. (It is 5·7 per cent of $L + 1·20$ ft). If the actual (i.e. measured) freeboard of a yacht is greater than the base freeboard for its L then there is a proportionate decrease in measured rating and a proportionate increase if it is lower than the base value. Low freeboards against base, however, are taxed at a higher rate (25 per cent compared to 15 per cent of difference) than higher ones are rewarded.

'Draft correction' follows the same principle – there is a base draft depending upon L. As we have seen in earlier chapters, deep draft is an advantage in a racing yacht especially when getting to windward. The IOR therefore establishes what it regards as a reasonable draft for a given sailing length – 14·6 per cent $L + 2·0$ ft, and then penalises the deeper drafts and rewards the shallower ones. IOR Mark III looks at draft in four categories of keel design – the fixed-keel yacht, the centreboard yacht, the drop-keel yacht, and the yacht with a 'movable appendage'. The fixed-keel yacht is one with a rudder on its keel or on a skeg but without a trimming tab on the keel which would make it a 'movable appendage' design. Fixed keels are simply taxed in accordance with the formula. Centreboards are restricted in weight, may not be ballasted and are restricted in their movement and positions. They have a special set of base drafts which cover the depth of the immersed body of the hull as well as that of the board. 'Drop keels' can be unlimited in weight but may move vertically up and down only. If they can be moved in any other direction they have to be locked in one position for measurement purposes and subsequently for racing. Moving appendages can be either the entire fixed keel operating like a slab rudder, a centreboard which can be trimmed across its box slightly to weather to increase its lift, a drop keel or some part of either a fixed keel, or a drop keel that can be moved like a trim tab. They are limited in weight and they carry a penalty of 0·75 per cent of measured rating.

The 'Engine and Propeller Factor' (EPF) was discussed briefly in chapter 4 and it is fairly straightforward. Three things are mandatory. One is that the engine shall be capable of driving the yacht at a speed/length ratio of at least $0·75/L^{\frac{1}{2}}$ in knots – note here the use of the calculated sailing length L – and, second, the propeller cannot be retracted or shielded other than by aperture or strut, third, there must be a means of locking the propeller when sailing. A point to note here is that whilst the main formula and the two corrections produce answers in feet (or metres), the EPF and the CGF, which we shall consider later, give their answers as percentage factors. The EPF may not be taken as less than 0·9600 (96 per cent) to guard against the fitting of very large engines. It is derived from the sum of the 'Engine

Moment Factor' (EMF) and the propeller 'Drag Factor' (DF). The EMF is the calculation of the contribution which the engine makes to the stability of the hull and its factors are engine weight and the horizontal distance of the centre of the cylinder block from the midpoint of LBG. Making the most out of EPF calls for fine judgement on gain in rating against possible loss in performance – the eternal twin horns of dilemma for all offshore designers. In most yachts, the midships position for the engine is the optimum, but by moving the engine forward it may be possible to gain slightly in rating without affecting performance. In some older yachts where the engine was aft, a new position forward may give a gain in both rating and in windward performance. The propeller factor depends upon the size and depth of the propeller and it is notable that the IOR expects two-bladed propellers only on racing craft. There is no allowance for three- and four-bladed ones.

As we saw in chapter 2, the stability of a yacht and hence its ability to carry sail depends upon the height of its centre of gravity. This in turn depends upon many other factors when heeled about the fore and aft axis like ballast ratio, beam, weight of the hull structure and the deck, weight of mast, etc. The CGF does not measure the height of the centre of gravity of a given hull directly but by employing an inclining test it establishes from the calculated righting moment at a small angle of heel (1°) a 'tenderness ratio' for the particular yacht. It is then possible using a graph to convert the tenderness ratio into a 'centre of gravity factor'. By adjusting the curve on the graph the rating authority can to some extent control the limits of 'tenderness' which it will permit. One of the changes from IOR Mark II to IOR Mark III was an adjustment upwards of the minimum value of CGF which was permitted from 0·9700 to 0·9850. This was intended to discourage extremely light or 'skinned out' boats, particularly those in the smaller offshore classes which depended to an excessive degree upon the stability provided by the crew sitting out on the weather rail. The CGF should have an optimum rating to performance value of about 1·0. Anything significantly higher means that the yacht has an unfavourably high rating. Markedly lower means that performance will suffer in stronger winds.

The inclining test used in assessing CGF is based on a well-established principle in naval architecture that is used for assessing the stability of large ships. The problem in yachts, especially small yachts, lies in measuring the small angles of transverse inclination involved without the measurer's own weight affecting the figures. Laboratory clinometers proved useless and the RORC measurers have devised a special 'manometer' – a device employing coloured liquid and tubing which enables values of heel not only to be read more accurately but to be read outside the hull and without anyone being aboard. This merely serves to illustrate the extent to which the efficacy of the IOR Mark III depends upon the devotion, integrity and ingenuity of the measurers.

These same qualities are called into use in protecting the validity of the rule from the various design devices which aim to make unnaturally large measurements of beam and depth. The artificial chine we have mentioned already. There is also the 'bucket' or bulge and sundry other bumps and corners which are pushed out of the hull in way of the depth measurement points. Measurers are charged that when 'hollows or projections or other deviations from the fair surface of the hull occur in the way of a point of measurement', measurers shall adjust the measurement back to what it should have been. The main difficulty here lies in insuring that two different measurers would come out with the same result.

The end product of the involved system of measurement and calculation under the IOR Mark III is a rating in feet or metres. As we have seen, with ratings being rounded to the nearest tenth of a foot, there is a restricted number of ratings between the IOR limits of 16–70 ft and already there is tendency for particular ratings to be adopted for specific boat-for-boat contests. Despite this development, which seems likely to continue in the future, the IOR Mark III is still required to permit yachts of widely differing sizes and types to race against each other. The problem therefore is, having arrived at a rating which approximates to the effective sailing length of the yacht, how to convert this to a handicap which we can apply against the time or distance of a specific race.

In the earlier chapters we saw that whilst the theoretical maximum speed of a yacht was given by $1\cdot5/L^{\frac{1}{2}}$, the average speed over the longer passages was usually no greater than $1\cdot0/L^{\frac{1}{2}}$. 'Rating' being assumed to be a better measure of actual sailing length than LWL, this could be written $1\cdot0/R^{\frac{1}{2}}$. We could then assume that, say, a yacht with a 25 ft *rating* would average 5 knots and one of 36 ft rating, 6 knots. We could then use this information in one of two ways. We could say that on a 300 mile race the 25 footer would take 60 hours and the 36 footer, 50 hours and that, therefore, the larger yacht should give the smaller one ten hours of elapsed time. For convenience we could convert this basic speed into the number of seconds taken to sail one nautical mile – 720 in the case of the small yacht and 600 in the case of the bigger – and the difference between these two values could be multiplied by the race distance to give time allowance. We would, in short, have a 'time-on-distance' system. On the other hand, we could say that the small boat would sail the same distance in 60 hours that the 36 footer would sail in 50 hours and a mythical 100 footer would sail in 30 hours. Thus if we multiplied the elapsed times taken on a race by a Time Correction Factor (TCF), 0·5, 0·6 and 1·0 respectively, each would take the same time. We would then have what is known as a 'time-on-time' system.

Both these systems would be primitive by modern standards although the time-on-distance method I have outlined was roughly that employed in the era of the 'tonnage' rule and by the early offshore races in the United States mentioned in chapter 5. With a little refinement to cover the range of yacht sizes more accurately, a very similar formula to the one I have suggested was used as the basis of the North American Yacht Racing Union's Time Allowance Table and the RYA Time on distance handicap system. The CCA used the NAYRU Table for all its major events. The RORC however always used the 'time-on-time' system for offshore races whereas the 'time-in-distance' system was usually employed for inshore events. (The conversion of TCF into seconds per nautical mile is a matter of simple division.)

Both systems have their deficiencies. The 'time-on-distance' method depends upon the distance sailed being the same as the distance of the race as planned. If there is a long plug to windward then an additional 50 miles or more may be added to the race distance and this will completely absorb handicap time differences and the smaller yachts will not stand a chance. If there is a full strong tide fair to the course then the race distance will be shorter and the little boats will have a birthday. The 'time-on-time' method depends for its part on the race being sailed at something like the assumed average speed. If the race hits a lot of calm, time goes by with the little boats collecting a tax-free bonus in corrected time from the larger ones who cannot hope to make it up. Alternatively, in fast downwind races the elapsed time differences between large and small yachts rapidly increase and the smaller yachts lose out. Both systems also suffer from the inevitable shortcoming that when we are dealing with wide variations in size and handicap the bigger boats rapidly leave the smaller ones behind and they are, certainly in British waters, soon sailing in markedly different conditions of wind and tide. Neither system is satisfactory in races with extremes of speed. So having modernised the rating rule into a highly precise instrument of performance measurement, the RORC set up a Time Allowance System Committee to study the problem of converting rating into a handicap system with enough flexibility to respond to the varying conditions encountered in a season of offshore races by a wide range of ratings of yachts. The result of their deliberations was the 'Performance Factor System' which the RORC introduced for the 1973 season after it had been tried out on the results of a lot of past races on both sides of the Atlantic and running it experimentally in parallel with the older RORC 'time-on-time' system for the 1972 season in the UK. It has not yet, however, been accepted for international events by the ORC.

Like the IOR Mark III itself, it is a combination of the two systems, the British favoured time-on-time and the United States preferred time-on-distance. The idea is to include in the calculations all the relevant factors in the race – distance, elapsed time, and rating. The basic formula looks like this:

Corrected Time = Elapsed Time — YRF (Distance Factor — Elapsed Time)

where YRF = Yacht Rating Factor.

Elapsed time is clearly only available when the yacht has finished the race but the rest of the ingredients can be pre-cooked before the race and corrected times worked out quickly after the finish. This perhaps is not ideal, but on this side of the Atlantic, at least, offshore crews are accustomed to the long silence between crossing the line and hearing the result. The distance factor is, in effect, a calculation of the slowest speed that the race could have been sailed and still have been a race at all. The formula is:

$$\text{Distance Factor} = \frac{\text{course rhumb line distance in n.m.}}{2 \cdot 75}$$

The magic figure of 2·75 knots has been arrived at because at speeds below that figure skin-friction accounts for the greater portion of the hull drag and the ratio of sail-area to wetted surface determines speed more than size and displacement. As we saw in chapter 2, it is the 'regime' where small boats and large boats sail at similar speeds and the onset of laminar flow over wetted surfaces is the main criterion – and quite unpredictable at the present state of knowledge. Furthermore, records show that in the history of the RORC there has never been a race where the leading boats have not bettered 2·75 knots average speed. (Some boats clearly have averaged lower speeds but, in this respect, bad boats like bad cases make bad law.)

The 'Time Correction Factor' is now called the 'Yacht Rating Factor' and is completely different from the old TCF which was derived from the RORC rating for the 'time-on-time' system. The formula used then was:

$$\text{TCF} = \frac{R^{\frac{1}{2}} + 2 \cdot 6}{10}$$

Now, as we have seen, the main fault of the 'time-on-time' system was that its fair application depended on the race being carried out at average speed proportional to a vee-over root L speed of about unity. No allowance could be made for fast races which favoured the bigger boats or slow races where the smaller yachts gained. The clue, of course, lies in the use of a fixed value of vee-over-root L or rating because fast races could be at $1\cdot5 \sqrt{R}$ and slow ones down at $0\cdot5 \sqrt{R}$. The addition of the constant to the fundamental expression was an attempt to tip the scales against a permanent balance in the system against the larger yachts. It was changed from time to time – until 1957 it was only 2 – but this adjustment could only ease rather than overcome the basic limitations of the system. The new system of calculating YRF ($=$ old TCF) is inevitably more complex. The formula is:

$$\frac{\dfrac{R^{\frac{1}{2}}}{R_s^{\frac{1}{2}}} - 1\cdot0}{\dfrac{1\cdot5\ R^{\frac{1}{2}}}{2\cdot75} - 1\cdot0} = \text{YRF},$$

where $R = $ IOR Mark III Rating: $R_s = $ IOR Mark III Rating of the 'scratch' boat. For the first season of the rule, the RORC decided that the 'scratch' rating should be 29 ft.

Turning figures into words, the new YRF can be explained as follows. The top line arrives at a factor which relates the yacht's average performance to that of the scratch boat. Boats bigger than the scratch boat will come out with a positive answer, those with a lower rating will come out with a negative answer. The numerator of the formula compares $1\cdot5\ R^{\frac{1}{2}}$ – the theoretical maximum speed of the yacht (*and* one which has never been exceeded in recorded RORC results) – with the race minimum which we discussed earlier, and arrives at what might be called a 'speed capability factor'. The simple act of dividing this speed capability factor into the relative rating factor gives a YRF which allows for relative size and potential performance. Depending upon the sign of the relative size factor it will be positive or negative which means that boats with ratings lower than the scratch boat will have a corrected time less than their elapsed time whereas boats with ratings higher than the scratch boat will add the correction to their elapsed time.

Let us look at some comparative figures for the IOR Mark III range of yachts. First, the new value of individual YRF. Although ratings remain an intelligible value and TCF was a fraction which converted elapsed time into corrected time by simple multiplication, YRF is not an immediately negotiable factor outside the confines of the formula I gave earlier. Individual values are therefore of little immediate value as comparators. The table at the head of the page opposite will show what I mean.

Applying these factors to previous race results the following gives an idea on how the shortcomings of the earlier RORC time-on-time should be rectified by the new Performance Factor system.

First, a slow race when, as we saw earlier, the bigger yachts lose so much corrected time to the smaller ones that they can never catch up. Such a race was the Bassurelle Race in 1971 (220 miles) when the first yacht home – *Quailo III* – took over 50 hours – an average speed of $4\cdot4$ knots or $V_s/R^{\frac{1}{2}} = 0\cdot69$, a speed/length ratio well down in the region where skin-friction accounts for the greater proportion of the total hull resistance – and also a factor not allowed for in the IOR formula. Although *Quailo*'s average speed was fastest in Class I – indeed in the fleet – she was placed fifth in her class on corrected time. (See second table on facing page.)

This would at least suggest that the balance against the bigger yachts in light airs and slow races has to some extent been redressed. In equity, the opposite must apply – do smaller

IOR Mark III Ratings

Yacht Rating Factors based on 29 ft rating scratch yacht

Rating (ft)	YRF
16	−0·2176
20	−0·1178
25	−0·0414
29	0·0000
30	+0·0086
35	+0·0443
40	+0·0712
45	+0·0924
50	+0·1099
55	+0·1239
60	+0·1359
65	+0·1463
70	+0·1554

Bassurelle Race, 1971

Order overall (TOT)		Order overall (PF)	
1	*Windsprite* (Class V)	1	*Morning Cloud* (Class II)
2	*Ballerina* (Class IV)	2	*Cervantes IV* (Class II) / *Windsprite* (Class V)
3	*Ossian III* (Class IV)	3	*Carillion* (Class I)
4	*Kealoha* (Class III)	4	*Quiver VI* (Class I)
5	*Cervantes IV* (Class II)	5	*Quailo III* (Class I)
6	*Morning Cloud* (Class II)		

yachts gain in fast, heavy-wind races? One such race was the 1972 Hook of Holland Race. This is what would have happened if TCF had been in use:

Hook of Holland Race, 1972

Order overall (TOT)		Order overall (PF)	
1	*Poinciana* (Class II)	1	*Angel* (Class IV)
2	*Belita VII* (Class II)	2	*Poinciana* (Class II)
3	*Flame* (Class II)	3	*Belita VII* (Class II)
4	*Angel* (Class IV)	4	*Mar del Norte* (Class IV)
5	*Polka Mazurka* (Class III)	5	*Jantine* (Class IV)
6	*Morning Town* (Class III)	6	*Polka Mazurka* (Class III)
7	*Standfast* (Class I)	7	*Flame* (Class III)

It would seem then that justice has been done to the poor! To round up this jobbing backwards on race results using the TCF system, let us look at the 1971 Fastnet. (See table on p. 114.)

Ragamuffin – the winner by both forms of reckoning – sailed the course at $V/R^{\frac{1}{2}} = 1\cdot12$, so this was a moderately fast race although it was marked by contrasting conditions. The way out to the Rock was marked by long periods of calm – *Carina*, for example, had to kedge

Fastnet Race, 1971

Order overall (TOT)		Rating	Order overall (PF)	Rating
1	Ragamuffin	39·5	Ragamuffin	39·5
2	Quailo III	40·7	American Eagle	55·1
3	Cervantes IV	29·5	Quailo III	40·7
4	American Eagle	55·1	Apollo	53·1
5	Yankee Girl	44·6	Yankee Girl	44·6
6	Improbable	37·7	Cervantes IV	29·5
7	Apollo	53·1	Carina	38·5
8	Bay Bea	40·2	Improbable	37·7
9	Noreyma VG	40·5	Bay Bea	40·2
10	Mersea Oyster	29·4	Noreyma VG	40·5
11	Standfast	33·0	Avra	39·1
12	Spinda	36·1	Spinda	36·1
13	Prospect of Whitby	33·2	Mersea Oyster	29·4
14	Avra	39·1	Standfast	33·0

off Start Point for 5 hours – followed by a hair-raising run back in Force 8 winds. In such conditions under the TOT system, as more time would be spent getting to the Rock – it is the longer leg anyway – than getting back, the smaller boats would be expected to benefit against the larger. This is apparent from the TOT results above. The performance factor system, however appears to have adjusted this artificial handicap hence the promotion of *American Eagle* and *Apollo*. But also of interest is the promotion of *Carina* – she was 15th under TOT – to 7th place and the demotion of *Cervantes* from 3rd to 6th. This suggests that the new system can be selective of inequities in size but does not always reward high average performance. *Cervantes* had the highest average $V/R^{\frac{1}{2}}$ at 1·14 and *Carina* the second at 1·13. They both lost out to the bigger yachts but were placed – on PF – side by side.

All this is of course highly theoretical and by the time this book is published we shall have experience of real results under the new system. Its mathematical origins appear to be impeccable and there is no doubt that it will be administered efficiently and justly. But....

The very complexity of the IOR Mark III and its associated time factor system – assuming that the system is universally adopted – give rise inevitably to serious misgivings about its practicability. In this, of course, it rivals Value Added Tax and like that tax, though in both cases there will be plenty of experts on hand to advise, lack of understanding gives rise to suspicion and suspicion to distrust. This is a serious matter for a sport like ocean-racing where the whole edifice depends to a very large extent upon mutual trust between the race organisers and participants. Skippers and crews are trusted to observe a host of rules, to go round all the marks and not yield to temptation and take short cuts. They are frequently trusted in recording their own finishing times and it is a mercifully rare event for the racing authorities to seek verification of any of these matters other than by the owner's word and a signature on the declaration form. For most people who race and probably even for all, there would be no point in racing at all if the rules meant nothing and the element of trust between the race authorities and the crews and between one crew and another was seriously jeopardised. But who outside the ranks of designers, mathematicians and computer operators can be sure he is getting a fair deal out of IOR Mark III and the Time Performance Factor system?

In this chapter I have not so far mentioned the immense problems of measurement under the IOR Mark III. There is a large volume of 'Instructions to Measurers' which carries into greater detail and depth the rules spelled out in the IOR Mark III itself. Yacht measurement as a profession nowadays vies with that of actuary for sheer wrangling complexity. No longer is it enough to have one's boat measured and 'there's an end of it'. Any change to sail, rig or trim and the almost incessant changes in the rule itself call for the services of the measurer. For many owners the rating arrived at is accepted as a fact, but, with the increasing use of fixed rating values in competition like the One Ton Cup, repeated alterations and adjustments are needed to get as close to the mandatory figure as possible. This does not mean just one visit from the measurer but several since, invariably, a computer run will be needed between each visit.

All this can also be seen in terms of extra cost in what is already an extremely costly sport – it is already being said that the cheapest way to build an ocean-racer nowadays is to make the hull out of papier maché using pound or dollar notes. For more than a decade it has been tacitly accepted that to have any chance at all in the major offshore events anywhere in the world required a new boat every other year. Ocean-racing under the IOR Mark III therefore, which has always attracted enthusiasts from both the well-heeled and the straitened, might begin to lose adherents just as the old larger metre-boat classes steadily diminished in the years after World War I. Already in the United Kingdom, there has been a steady reduction since World War II first in the size of yacht qualifying for Class I and more recently in the numbers of such yachts as a whole compared with the expansion of the off-shore fleet as a whole. It becomes increasingly difficult for Club and corporately owned boats to compete and the erstwhile offshore institution of the owner-designed and built giant-killer like FAEM and PEN AR BED has virtually disappeared. The very introduction of the IOR has effectively made obsolete a vast number of yachts which still possess the capability for many years of sailing in offshore events. Already too, as this book is being written, there is a growing call for a 'better deal' for the older yachts in the RORC programme. All this echoes an earlier epoch in yachting history – the introduction of the IYRU rule in the earlier years of the century. Then a group of disenchanted yachtsmen set up the 'Boat Racing Association' and, as we saw in the last chapter, such break-away factions have been a feature of the history of the game. History may not repeat itself but there is a pattern in the affairs of great institutions which has a recurrent quality.

Earlier in this chapter I described the IOR Mark III as the 'space-age' comparator and in this respect it reflects the immensely technical times we live in. It is already inspiring a new breed of yachts as we shall see in the next chapter. But crews win races, not boats, and it will be the extent to which it succeeds in eliminating the boat from the race-winning equation that will determine its success or failure over the years.

7

The Way Ahead for Yachts

Throughout this book so far we have been looking at yachts in the past tense and seeking to discover how scientific discovery and technical development in both design and in the all-pervasive rating rules have influenced the shape and appearance of hulls and sail plans. In this chapter we shall take a look into the future and see if we can discern even a glimmer of the shape of yachts to come. Many people will say that such a task is impossible because rating rules may change, there may be a scientific discovery tomorrow which will enable us all to sail directly into the wind or else, perhaps, that yacht development has reached the ultimate plateau of progress and there is little further to go. Finally, some will add that it is not given to man to foretell the future and any attempt to do so is merely idle and valueless speculation.

No one can deny the truth of much of this but at this stage in our technical history there are many thousands of people who spend their working lives thinking very seriously about the future and seeking to lift the hem of that particular curtain just a little. Suppose we were dealing with aeroplanes instead of yachts. The lead-time from conception to entry into service there would be about ten times that of a yacht. Someone therefore has to cast his mind forward over the whole of that dimly seen decade and predict the outcome of an immense range of technological factors, design trends and developments in ancillary fields. Shipbuilders, especially naval shipbuilders, face similar problems. The wonder is not so much that sometimes it is done badly but that very frequently it is done well. There is, of course, a technique.

One such technique is to endeavour to discern trends of development and then project them – extrapolate is the right word here – into the future. The difficulty lies first of all in analysing the trends and next in assessing the rate of change in the future. As students of stock-market charts will know, there are at least three trends to be considered. Primary trend is the deep ground swell of development – the longstanding tendencies of things to change relentlessly but perhaps quite slowly over a period of decades rather than years. Secondary trends are of shorter duration and tend to fluctuate in direction perhaps over periods of one or two years. Tertiary trends are of short duration subject to rapid small changes and their influence is momentary. In seamen's language, the groundswell, the wave pattern and the ripples. In terms of yacht design, a definite primary trend has been for offshore yachts to get smaller in size; a secondary trend might be the popularity of masthead rig; a tertiary trend is probably the bustle. Let us first look at some of the primary and secondary trends evident at the moment and then go on and see how all three seem likely to influence the shape of yachts to come.

Looking back over the last few decades there is clear evidence that in terms of size, yachts making up the RORC fleets have steadily been getting smaller. The reasons are almost certainly the rising cost of each ton Thames both in building and maintenance and less obviously, the virtual disappearance of the professional 'paid-hand' to help out with maintenance and sail handling. Class I of the RORC has steadily declined in numbers and required its lower limit to be reduced to keep the class alive. *Myth of Malham* for example was originally in Class II but was promoted into Class I when the class divisions were revised in 1961. (She celebrated her elevation by winning the Class I Championship in that year with the same facility as she had won the Class II Championship for the previous five years.) To pick out the 'average yacht' is like picking out the average man – they come in all shapes and sizes – but looking at the better performers of each period, there has been a reduction in LOA from about 50 ft to 55 ft in the late 1930s when the purpose-designed ocean racer was becoming established to around 35–40 ft today. There is however some indication that sizes may be beginning to increase again and such yachts as the former America's Cup contestant the 12 metre *American Eagle* – 67 ft LOA – and *Windward Passage* – 73 ft LOA – appearing on the scene may be heralding an increase in average size. It can also be argued that until the adoption of the RORC's performance factor system of time allowance which was examined in chapter 6, the handicapping system, at least in British waters, favoured the smaller boat. At the same time, economic and crewing factors seem likely still to impose an upper limit on yacht size and there seems little likelihood of any yacht of 47 tons qualifying for the description given to 'gallant little *Aurora*' in 1851.

Average yachts are even harder to define statistically. The best we can do – short of several thousand pounds worth of computer time – is to select for each era a yacht which appears to typify the dominant design. Since, as I explained in the first chapter, winners tend to constitute the breeding stock, our exemplars are also required to be winners. The following Table is an attempt to codify the process of natural selection since the offshore-racer became a design in its own right.

Period	Yacht	$\dfrac{\text{LWL}}{B}$	$\dfrac{W}{((\text{LWL})/100)^3}$	Ballast ratio	$\text{SA}/W^{\frac{1}{3}}$	$\dfrac{\text{SA}}{\text{LWL}}$
Workbook era	*Jolie Brise* (1895)	3·0	500	—	180	53
Early US	*Dorade* (1930)	3·5	290	—	190	31
Early British	*Ortac* (1937)	3·2	325	—	180	28
Light displacement era	*Myth of Malham* (1947)	3·6	200	—	165	19
Late British traditional	*Belmore* (1958)	2·8	440	39%	165	26
US RORC challenge	*Clarion of Wight* (1963)	2·8	415	45%	158	24
UK RORC response	*Quiver IV* (1964)	2·9	333	48%	165	28
Late RORC	*Morning Cloud I* (1969)	2·4	322	44%	178	20
Early IOR	*Noreyma VIII* (1971)	2·9	230	47%	182	27
IOR Mark III	*Swan 44* (1972)	2·8	240	45%	180	25

* Denotes GRP construction.

The trends indicated here would suggest that there is a clear primary trend for beam/length ratios to get less – or for boats to become beamier – but that of recent years the trend has flattened out with a value of around 3:1 with secondary movements fluctuating between 2·5:1 and the mean value. These secondary movements – the obvious one is the increase in LWL/B with the introduction of the IOR Mark II – result from the interplay of rating factors. Does this then suggest that we may once again see beam/length ratios rising? We shall be examining some of the more speculative designs to IOR Mark III later in this chapter but at the present juncture in the life of this infant rule it is difficult to be certain whether it will spawn thin boats or fat boats.

When we look at the relationship between LWL and displacement the primary trend seems clearer. Displacement for each foot of waterline length has steadily been reducing over a considerable period with the introduction of lighter methods of safe, strong construction. The introduction of GRP tended to accelerate the trend and we may expect the increasing use of aluminium to continue it to values of 200 or less. (It is worth remembering here that *Myth* at 200 was by no means an excessively 'light displacement' yacht. *Black Soo* which could plane under ideal conditions had a mean density of 61 and even *Mouse of Malham*, which was more of an all-rounder than *Black Soo*, had 174.) We can therefore expect, I believe, to see mean displacement densities of the order of 180–200 in the near future.

Ballast ratios over the longer term have also steadily increased but they too seem now to be levelling off at around 45 per cent. It may be that in other connections we shall see a tendency for a breakaway from the fixed keel – we shall discuss the reasons shortly – to some form of adjustable keel. This could mean that ballast ratios will tend to be reduced again and this tendency may serve to arrest that towards less beam, a reminder again that all these design factors are closely inter-related.

The other two ratios – sail-area to displacement and sail-area to waterline length – are not indicating any particular trend. The fluctuation in $SA/W^{\frac{1}{3}}$ is comparatively slight and the figure for sail-area per foot of LWL varies with the density of the hull rather than its length. Where this latter figure may be of significance is in the virtually unobtainable ratio of sail-area to wetted surface but it is clear here that the heavier displacement yachts will gain. Apart, however, from the light airs performance factor we would not expect much change in the future in either value.

Throughout this book I have repeatedly stressed the influence of the rating rule on design criteria. In previous chapters I have tried to show how the objective of the rating rule has been over the years to achieve a practical estimate of actual sailing length. That this is a matter of the utmost complexity should at least be clear! There is therefore no thoroughly dependable way of looking at design tendencies relating to the rating rules without a systematic dissection of each of the rating factors for each sample yacht. This again would mean the use of computer time, and out of place in a book of this type. What we can do, however, is make two assumptions. They are that the rating rule of the day arrives at an estimate of the effective sailing length of each yacht based on the best available technical means of the time and, second, that the LOA of a yacht is the absolute limit of its effective sailing length – bustles, *et al.* notwithstanding. Going back to the RORC Rule era, the more successful yachts usually had ratings about 90 per cent of their LWL. *Myth* for example was 90 per cent LWL at her later rating of 30·25 ft; *Belmore* was 90 per cent, *Danegeld* 87 per cent and *Clarion of Wight* 88 per cent. Under the IOR regime to date, persistent winners are those whose rating is the same or slightly lower than their LWL. Typical examples here are *Prospect of Whitby* rating 33·02 on 33·3 ft LWL, *Carillion* with a rating of 32·9 on a LWL of 33 ft. In Class II, *Morning Cloud II* rated 30·7 on 31·2 ft and in Class III, *Kealoha* (a Sparkman & Stephens-designed Swan 37) rating 27·4 on a LWL of 27·4 beat another Swan 37, *Tessanda*, for the points championship in 1972 and *Tessanda* rated 27·7 for the same LWL. In Class IV in 1972, the first three boats were of the same S & S design and in each case the LWL and the rating were almost identical – 24·6 rating on 24·1 LWL. None of this, of course, is intended to suggest that if someone produces a yacht which rates a foot less than LWL it will be a certain winner. The implication is that if a yacht rates appreciably higher than her LWL she may be over-rated and it would at least be worthwhile looking at her rating parameters critically again. It also suggests that for the future we should expect rating and LWL to be virtually identical. It is ironic perhaps that after a mountain of arithmetical calculations the final outcome should be, simply, that IOR Mark III rating = LWL!

We can now round up the various trends we have been able to discern so far. The trend-setters – Admiral's Cup and Onion Patch Trophy contestants – may tend to be slightly larger than today – perhaps roughly in the middle of the Class I bracket of 33–70 ft rating at 50 ft LWL and 50 ft rating. This would give us an average LOA of about 66 ft. Assuming that aluminium construction is likely to be used, the length/displacement ratio could be down to 180 or less and this would give a displacement of about 23 tons with a sail area of 1350 square feet giving 27 square feet to the foot or a sail-area/displacement ratio of 165. Already there are yachts not far removed from these dimensions appearing in American waters. We may yet see them in British on the not unreasonable assumption that development follows the precedents of the past. But what if it doesn't? Where are the most likely technical advances going to occur?

There seem to me to be three 'areas' of yacht performance where technical improvement seems likely to be sought. The first is in the reduction of wetted surface and its corollary, the reduction of skin-friction. The second is in the field of masting and rigging and the third in the reduction of hull windage.

As we saw in chapter 2, the fin keel contributes markedly to the total wetted surface of the hull and in the light airs case may cause a light displacement hull literally to 'stick' to the water: like sticky tape, the bigger the area the better the adhesion. Yet the fin keel is only needed when the wind is forward of the beam and there is an element of side force to be countered. On the other hand, there is an increasing requirement in lighter displacement hulls of the type we are anticipating of getting the ballast low. What we may expect to see therefore is increasing use of the drop-ballast keel. There are already a number in service – *Noreyma VII* or VG (Variable Geometry) has a keel lifted by hydraulics and could vary her profile to suit the prevailing conditions. She was RORC Class I champion in 1970, her first season, and fifth in her second. Similarly the end of the 1972 season saw the emergence on the other side of the Atlantic of *Salty Goose*, a yacht designed with a density $W/((LWL)/100)^3$ of 136. She also has a deep-draft, high-aspect 1:1 ratio keel which weighs 13,000 lb. Further features aimed at reducing wetted surface are her narrow beam – up to 3·9 LWL/B – and her slack bilges and fine ends. These are clearly signs of things to come.

They are also, however, trends which are already apparent and in many cases are no more than a modern version of something which has been tried before. If we think in terms of a breakthrough the most promising field is in reducing surface friction by inducing a flow régime like that of laminar flow which offers a tenfold reduction in hull drag over the more usual turbulent flow. But how to do it? Mechanical methods of delaying the break-away into turbulent flow by sucking the surface layer into the hull are already known but since they require the use of power they are not applicable to sailing yachts. It is also possible to drip soluble long-chain polymers from the bows of moving vessels and achieve a marked reduction in surface drag but this method too is unacceptable to offshore racing authorities and is likely to be too highly expensive even in Class I. There remains therefore the introduction of an entirely new bottom surface finish which by its nature would be inert and would not involve the emission of some lubricant substance or the use of external power. Already a study of porpoises has led to proposals that a flexible outer skin with an insulation of a suitable captive fluid between it and the outer hull would reduce the onset of turbulence. The next few years may therefore bring developments in this direction. The problem will be, as ever, that if the new outer layer reduces skin-friction at speeds of $V/L^{\frac{1}{2}} = 0.7$ and below, what will it do to wave resistance at higher speeds? It is worth recalling here however that we still spend the greater portion of time at lower speeds and 1 knot gained on 2 is a better investment than 1 knot gained on 7. So some change in hull surfaces is worth investigating. Having watched the way in which furred animals like seals and otters seem to be able to slip through the water I have often wondered whether a velvet finish to a yacht's bottom might not after all be a better answer than a high polish. Clearly there is much work to be done in this field – and as much in the interest of merchant ships as of yachts – and a great deal is undoubtedly being done at present. It can therefore be only a matter of time before something new emerges.

In chapter 3 I compared the performance of a glider aerofoil with that of a yacht sail as a measure of their relative efficiencies – something of the order of 10 to 1 in favour of the glider. Though we cannot ever hope to approach this order of efficiency in soft sails on real boats because of the 'interface' problem, we could do better if we could eliminate some of the major sources of parasite drag from the mast, rigging and sails *and* from the hull and the crew. We shall look at the aerodynamic drag from the rigging separately from that of hull and crew but they are, in fact, connected. Off the wind the air resistance of the hull and the crew above deck may actually contribute to increased driving force as will the air resistance of the mast and rigging. Whatever gain that arises from these sources, however, is completely offset in the offshore 'round trip' case by the reduction in performance to windward caused by the same parasitic drag. On the wind, the hull, if properly shaped, contributes to sail efficiency because it serves when heeled to close the gap between the boom and the surface of the sea and reduce the induced drag caused by the 'end effects' over the mainsail. At all events, it pays to have the boom as close to the deck as possible and unlike some of the proposals I shall discuss later, there is no rating limitation on the *minimum* height of 'Boom Above Deck' (BAD) under IOR Mark III. The limitation is on the upper end – BAD must not exceed, without penalty, $0.05P + 4.0$ ft.

Any real saving in parasite drag from the mast and rigging can only come from a new concept of mast design. What is required is a free-standing mast without rigging other than the forestay which itself might be solid. This would undoubtedly call for a thicker mast section particularly in the lower part but there is really no reason why we should not go back to mounting the mast on the keel. Indeed, the mast could even be an extension of the structural backbone of the yacht as could the forestay. It will also be necessary to consider the use of new materials like resin-bonded carbon filaments which have a tensile strength and modulus of elasticity as much as six times that of the alloys at present in use. The same material has already been used for spinnaker poles and booms with a considerable saving in weight. The prospect of a free-standing mast without shrouds, backstays or crosstrees would have benefits quite apart from the saving in air resistance which would result. To exploit the full value of such a development, however, it would be necessary to develop further the basic idea of the hybrid 'wing' sail.

The wing-sail principle is already being employed on both sides of the Atlantic to a limited extent with the introduction of various methods of shielding and streamlining the forestay and the headsail luff attached to it. The grooved forestay is one such system; another more promising one is the 'Head Foil' for which the designer claims a two degree improvement in the ability to point and, in theory, (V_{mg} measurements are notoriously difficult to obtain) an improvement in V_{mg} in average conditions of the order of 0·2 knots over an ordinary hanked-on genoa. There is a slight snag in making headsail changes with the device fitted but these may be overcome with further development. The main point here is that design interest is already becoming focused on obtaining higher aerodynamic efficiency from the sail plan by improving the leading edges. Furthermore, realising the implication for progress in design, the ORC decided to allow solid forestays but the penalty is that twice the width (or the greatest dimension in cross-section) is added to LP – the longest perpendicular of the headsail.

The true 'wing sail' I am referring to here is a development of the mainsail where the mast, free to rotate, constitutes the leading edge of the mainsail aerofoil and perhaps 30 per cent of its chord. Such an idea is rank heresy under the terms of the present IOR Mark III, and there is a great deal of development work to be done on the idea. But, as I have tried repeatedly to show in this book, continuous technical development in the face of either changeable rules or apparently purblind prejudice has been the hallmark of ocean-racing since its inception. Had it not been we should still be carrying sea-anchors and oil bags.

As is clear from many of the latest designs to the IOR Mark III appearing for the 1973 season, as this book is being completed, designers are now fully alert to the need to reduce hull and crew parasitic drag – the aerodynamic variety concerns us here – by numerous innovations. Decks have become flusher in recent years and the dog house has all but disappeared. Some designers accept the crew drag by requiring the crew to work on deck rather than in the cockpit, thereby reducing the size of the cockpit and the drag-creating eddies it can make. Others take the opposite view – notably the brilliantly successful American Dick Carter who is the only man to have won two Fastnets with yachts to his own design since Rod Stephens in *Dorade*. He has set up a system of linked 'ant hills' – an 'ant hill' is defined as a winching position with a handle but no winch barrel – in the cockpit where crews can work winch handles and tail sheets over winches separately. He has also run all his halliards through tubes under the deck to the cockpit. In his Canada's Cup design he also abolished the toe rail, deck cleats and the spinnaker boom track. And if we look around the topsides, the deck, and the mast assembly there are numerous small eddy-creating excrescences which can be either fined down or dispensed with altogether – cross-tree roots, shroud attachment points, spinnaker cups are examples, massive deck fittings and hatch covers standing too proud are others. We cannot yet, perhaps, afford to dispense with life-lines in favour of a sophisticated safety-belt system but we could have a look at the aerodynamic shape of the stanchions and its relation to the close-hauled position. The familiar 'whistle-buoy' noise most of them make is all too often the mating call of the air drag parasite!

Rather more complex, but no less essential, is the need in my view of a careful look at the hull's wind profile. By this I mean the shape the hull presents to the apparent wind when close-hauled with some lee-way and up to, say, 25° of heel. Here, as will be remembered from chapter 3, the 'cod's head and mackerel tail' shape offers appreciably less air drag than does the 'wedge'. We are inevitably up against the inherent 'interface problem' of compromising between the best shape for the water and the best for the air. It will be unusual too if the 'wind profile' is as simple as either of the basic hull shapes. What can be done is to smooth out sharp changes to the airflow over the hull by the judicious use of tumble-home and, perhaps, a knuckle at the forward end of the sheer strake. (In the latter case it will clearly also be necessary to watch the rating implications of paragraph 302, IOR Mark III.)

So much then for the trends in hull shape we think can be predicted. A less easy prediction to make is that of the development of rigs and sail plans. The main reason here is the 'horses for courses' factor I have referred to before. This factor also affects hull shape to some extent – the choice for example of a higher prismatic coefficient for a hull which is likely to be sailed in strong free winds than for one which spends most of its time on the wind. Such hull shapes are likely to be rather specialised extremes and hence a little apart from the main international offshore competition which serves as the main selection machinery for designs that will survive and multiply. With sail plans, however, the choice of single mast or schooner, yawl or ketch is greatly influenced by the waters in which most of the yacht's racing will be done. In British waters it is difficult to see that the single-masted rig is likely to be superseded in the near future because windward sailing tends to be the norm and the reduction of windage a continuous pre-occupation with designers and skippers. If we ever do get the unstayed mast, however, it may, at least at the outset, be easier to produce two slightly shorter masts than one single-stick and a 'free-standing' schooner would be an attractive proposition. In short, therefore, the next major step in rig design would seem to lie in the area already discussed – the improvement of masting from the 'biplane' to the 'monoplane' era.

As it happens, IOR Mark III has already produced a new rig – the cat-rigged ketch. ('Cat-rigged' means rigged with a mast virtually in the bow and no foretriangle and headsail.) The most interesting example is an American design *Cascade*. She has what are virtually two mainsails with booms flown from masts mounted virtually at the forward end of the waterline and slightly aft of amidships. Her main achievement appears to have been that she had slipped under the rating rule with a remarkable rating of 22·0 ft on a LWL of 30 ft. At the time of writing, however, there is no indication that this type of rig (see Fig 17) has any technical advantage other than ease of handling. It may simply be a rule-beater and the alacrity with which the ORC placed an immediate 10 per cent penalty on such yachts and hinted at more to come would appear to confirm this belief.

There have, however, also been other rigs which indicate that the field of inventiveness and experiment is still wide open under the IOR Mark III. One such example is the yacht *Equation* designed by the American designer, Britton Chance. She has a number of unusual hull features but her rig was of the greatest interest. She is ketch rigged and special consideration has been given to the effectiveness of the mizzen – our old friend the drag parasite – by giving it 'Gretel'-type folding spreaders so that the mizzen genoa can be carried up to 35° on the apparent wind. The mizzen mast can also be tilted upwind to avoid the backwash from the mainsail. The distance between the two masts is unusually large – again to reduce backwinding.

The Australian-designed *Ginkgo* and *Apollo II* – both by Bob Miller and third and fourth in the 1973 Sydney–Hobart Race – are also showing innovations in both hull and rig. Dealing with rig first, *Ginkgo* is a masthead sloop – against a recent trend in Australian waters towards cutter rig influenced by Fastnet winner *Ragamuffin* – with a high aspect ratio foretriangle and mainsail achieved by setting the mast slightly more forward than is now customary. (The luff/foot ratio is over 3 : 1.) The mast has internal rigging and faired in fittings and the designer has paid particular attention to reducing windage by eliminating as many mast-borne excrescences as possible. Significantly, the main boom is carried as close to the deck as is practicable. The hull shape is also unusual – virtually the old 'cod's head and mackerel tail' with the maximum beam well forward of amidships, deep and full bow sections with a finely tapering

LOA   37'6"
LWL   30'0"
Beam   12'3"
Draft   6'9"
Displacement   17,000 lbs.
Ballast   8,800 lbs.
Sail Area (main and mizzen)   570 sq. ft.
Power   Westerbeke 4-107
IOR Rating   22.0
Builder   Allan H. Vaitses
Designer:
    Jerome H. Milgram
    2 Kelly Road, Cambridge, Massachusetts

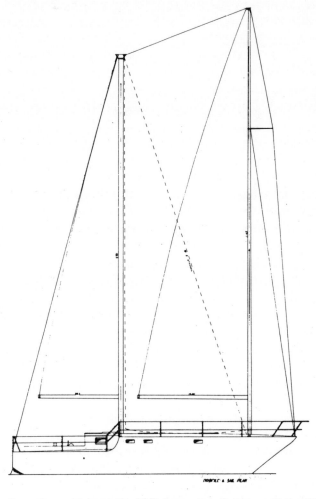

Cascade — which set the IOR dovecotes aflutter until the ORC imposed a rating penalty on such unusual designs. The cause of long-term yacht development appears unlikely to be adversely affected.

FIG 17   *The cat-rigged ketch.*

Yacht	Designer	LOA	LWL	LWL/B Ratio	W (tons)	Ballast ratio	$\dfrac{W}{\left(\dfrac{LWL}{100}\right)^3}$	$\dfrac{RSAT}{W^{\frac{1}{3}}}$	IOR rating	C'tion
ONE TONNERS:										
Munequita (Ranger 37)	Gary Mull	37·0	28·3	2·5	6·8	48%	295	175	27·5	GRP
Lightnin'	S & S	38·5	28·8	2·4	6·9	48%	280	175	,,	GRP
Robin	Ted Hood	35·0	28·5	2·7	6·2	45%	260	175	,,	GRP
Witchcraft	Bill Lee	35·0	27·0	2·5	3·4	33%	170	280	,,	Light alloy
Chance 33/29	Britton-Chance	33·0	29·0	3·1	6·1	53%	250	160	,,	GRP
Ydra	Dick Carter	37·0	29·0	2·4	6·8	40%	280	230·	,,	GRP
ADMIRAL'S CUP										
Gingko*	Bob Miller	45·5	41·0	3·4	10·3	55%	150	180	36·3	GRP
Salty Goose	Bob Derector	54·0	47·5	3·8	13·9	55%	130	200	44·6	Light alloy
Morning Cloud (III)	S & S	45·0	34·1		12·3	48%	315			Wood strip
Revolution	Finot	37·0	28·0	2·2					29·8	Light alloy
Charisma	S & S	55·6	40·0	2·8					44·2	Light alloy
Equation	Britton-Chance	68·4	57·5	3·7	25·8	48%	135	172	58·5	Light alloy
Norlin 34 (No-Go V)	Peter Norlin	33·8	26·7	2·4	4·45	56%	220	200	25·5	GRP

* APOLLO is a sister ship in light alloy

stern. In addition to a moderate bustle, the lines of the stern run naturally aft of the transom to induce the effect of greater length. *Gingko* is of laminated timber construction sheathed with Dynel-epoxy; her sister ship *Apollo II* is of duralmium. They rate 37 ft on a 41 ft LWL.

Another yacht which appears to have the aura of greatness about her at the time of writing is the Carter-designed *Ydra*, which through bad luck during the major offshore event was narrowly beaten for the 1973 One Ton Cup by another Carter-designed yacht, *Wai-Aniwa*. *Ydra*, two years the younger and very much IOR Mark III, is markedly different from her stable-mate, and these differences indicate how the rule changes have influenced one eminent designer. *Wai-Aniwa* is virtually 'cod's head and mackerel tail' – full forward and rounded with a long slack run aft. *Ydra* is broad beamed with her B_{max} well aft and straight waterlines in her forebody. Her stern shape too is different, being lower in profile and broader athwartships. Her rig is tall and narrow with an aspect ratio better than 3:1.

These then are two boats which might be the progenitors of the IOR Mark III breed. There are of course others still to be revealed for the coming Admiral's Cup and the Onion Patch contests. The yachts I have mentioned may, of course, be no more than flashes in the offshore pan or ripples on the groundswell of evolving design. It could also well be that the more conventional designs improving slowly will be the survivors. Alternatively, the pendulum could swing the other way and instead of the lighter stripped-out type of cruiser-racer dominating the scene, we could see a return to the heavy displacements of the past. My guess can be no better than anyone else's. I am therefore concluding this book with a table of the main design features of a selection of promising yachts as seen or reported at the onset of the first post-IOR Mark III season. From this information, and on the assumption that designers will get the crews their designs deserve, you, dear reader, must make your own choice of the trend-setter for the future. You will I hope have learned enough from these pages to compare, contrast and judge for yourself. This introductory lesson on comparative yacht anatomy is ended.

Bibliography
and References

HISTORY

HEATON, Peter. *Yachting – a History* (1955)
LOOMIS, Alfred E. *Ocean Racing 1866–1935* (New York 1967)
MARTIN, E. G., and IRVING, John. *Cruising and Ocean Racing* (1934)
PHILLIPS-BIRT, Douglas. *An Eye for a Yacht* (1955)
——. *British Ocean Racing* (1960)

DESIGN AND DEVELOPMENT

BARNABY, K. C. *Basic Naval Architecture* (1953)
HARRISON BUTLER, T. *Cruising Yachts: Design and Performance* (1958)
ILLINGWORTH, John. *Offshore* (Various eds)
KAY, H. F. *The Science of Yachts, Wind and Water* (1971)
KINNEY, F. S. *Skene's Element of Yacht Design* (1962)
MARCHAJ, C. A. *Sailing Theory and Practice* (1964)
PHILLIPS-BIRT, Douglas. *Sailing Yacht Design* (1951, 1971)
——. *Naval Architecture of Small Craft* (1957)

RATING RULES AND HANDICAP SYSTEMS

HOLLINGSWORTH, Alan. *Crewing Offshore* (1964)
JOHNSON, Peter. *Yachtsman's Guide to the Rating Rule* (1971)

YACHT CONSTRUCTION

Rules and Regulations of Lloyd's Register of Shipping for the Construction and Classification of Yachts
    Vol I   *Wood and Composite Yachts*
    Vol II   *Steel Yachts*
    Vol III *Yachts of the International Rating Classes*
    Provisional Rules for the Construction of Reinforced Plastic Yachts
Lloyd's Register of Yachts

WATTS, C. J. *Practical Yacht Construction* (1957)

Appendix A
Comparative Yacht
Anatomy 1850-1973

Typical Yachts and their Performance Criteria

Year	Yacht	Designer	LWL (ft)	W (tons)
1850	*America*	Steers	90·3	146
1895	*Jolie Brise*	Paumelle	48	55
1931	*Dorade*	Stephens	37	15
1937	*Ortac*	Clark	35	14
1947	*Myth of Malham*	Laurent Giles	33·5	7·6
1955	*Carina*	Rhodes	36·5	14
1956	*Mouse of Malham*	Illingworth	24	2·4
1957	*Black Soo*	Van de Stadt	29·5	1·6
1958	*Belmore*	Illingworth	26·5	8·4
1959	*Danegeld*	Cheverton	24·0	5·6
1963	*Clarion of Wight*	Sparkman Stephens	30·0	10·0
1964	*Quiver IV*	Camper & Nicholson	35	14·3
1966	*Clarionet*	S & S	36·9	6·4
1969	*Morning Cloud (I) SS 34*	S & S	24·2	4·5
1970	*Kealoha (Swan 37)*	S & S	27·4	6·9
1970	*Windward Passage*	Alan Gurney	65	35·5
1971	*Carillion of Wight*	S & S	33·0	10·8
1971	*Noreyma VIII (Swan 48)*	S & S	36·0	13·5
1972	*Swan 44*	S & S	35·2	10·6

SA (sq ft)	$\dfrac{W}{((L)/100)^3}$	$\dfrac{SA}{W^{2/3}}$	LWL/R (%)	Ballast Ratio	$\dfrac{LWL}{B}$	AR Keel*	Rig	AR† Main	AR† Fore Δ
5263	200	190		32%	4:1	·55	Gaff Schooner	1·1:1	1·2:1
2600	500	180		30%	3:1	·68	Gaff Cutter	1·6:1	1·6:1
1150	290	190		35%	3.5:1	·90	Bermuda yawl	2:1	2·7:1
965	325	180		35%	3·2:1	·83	Sloop	2·3:1	2·8:1
625	200	165	90%	51%	3·6:1	·83	Cutter	3·1:1	3·16:1
1194	289	206		CB	2·8:1		Yawl	2·6:1	3·1:1
260	174	144		39%	3:1	2·0	Yawl	3·2:1	4·2:1
730	61	540	90%		3·8:1	2·0	Sloop		
680	440	165	90%	39%	2·8:1	·70	Sloop	2·8:1	2·8:1
446	400	138	87%		2·5:1		Sloop		
725	415	158	88%	45%	2·8:1		Sloop		
972	333	165		48%	2·9:1		Sloop		
512	337	140	102%	48%	2·7:1		Sloop		
483	322	178	105%	44%	2·4:1	2·0	Sloop	4·0:1	2·8:1
598	330	165	100%	48%	2·5:1	2·0	Sloop	3·5:1	3·0:1
2437	135	225			3·4:1		Ketch		
729	300	147	99%	50%	2·5:1		Sloop		
1032	230	182	100%	47%	2·9:1	2·0	Sloop	3·3:1	3·1:1
875	240	180	95%	45%	2·8:1	2·0	Sloop	3·2:1	3·0:1

* Aspect ratio is calculated on the basis of $\dfrac{\text{Draft}^2}{\text{Keel Area}}$.

† These are luff/foot ratios.

Appendix B
Some Historic Performances

The times in the following table are not record-breaking performances. They are included here to show how even over a period of one hundred years, 'round trip' speeds in terms of speed/length ratios have not altered appreciably.

TRANSATLANTIC

Year	Yacht (LOA)	Route	Distance (nm)	Time (days)	$V/L^{\frac{1}{2}}$
1866	*Henrietta* (107)	Sandy Hook–Needles	3100	13	·96
1870	*Cambria* (108)	Daunt Rock–Sandy Hook	2900	23	·51
1887	*Coronet* (133)	New York–Ireland	2900	15	·70
1905	*Atlantic* (185)	Sandy Hook–Lizard	3000	12	·77
1928	*Nina* (59)	New York–Santander	3300	24	·74
1931	*Dorade* (52)	Newport–Plymouth	2800	17	·96
1935	*Stormy Weather* (53)	Newport–Bergen	3100	19	·93
1948	*Myth of Malham* (38)	Bermuda–Brixham	3010	22	·95
1952	*Samuel Pepys* (30)	Bermuda–Plymouth	2900	25	1·05
1957	*Carina* (53)	Newport–Santander	3100	18	·99
1963	*Ondine* (58)	Annapolis–Lizard	3000	18	·89
1972	*Noreyma VIII* (48)	Bermuda–Bayona	2800	20	·86

FASTNET

Year	Yacht (LWL)	Distance (nm)	Time (hrs)	$V/L^{\frac{1}{2}}$
1925	*Jolie Brise* (48)	615	145	·58
1928	*Nina* (50)	615	110	·79
1935	*Stormy Weather* (39)	585	114	·82
1948	*Myth of Malham* (33·5)	605	132	·80
1955	*Carina* (36·5)	605	104	·93
	Mouse of Malham	605	139	·89
1963	*Clarion of Wight* (30)	605	121	·91
1961	*Rabbit* (30)	605	115	·96
1967	*Pen Duick III* (30)	605	88	1·25
1969	*Red Rooster* (32·5)	605	113	·93
1971	*Ragamuffin* (36)	605	86	1·18

BERMUDA

Year	Yacht (LWL)	Distance (nm)	Time (hrs)	$V/L^{\frac{1}{2}}$
1906	*Tamerlane* (31)	660	126	·94
1933	*Highland Light* (50)	660	72	1·30
1972	*Noreyma VIII* (39)	660	108	·98

HONOLULU

Year	Yacht (LWL)	Distance (nm)	Time (hrs)	$V/L^{\frac{1}{2}}$
1906	*Lurline* (72)	2300	298	·91
1971	*Windward Passage* (65)	2225	225	1·23

Appendix C The International Offshore Rule Mark III

ALPHABETICAL INDEX OF SYMBOLS IN THE RULE

Abbrev	No.	Description
FIGS	311	Forward inner girth station
FM	403	Freeboard measured
FMD	328	Freeboard at MDS
FOC	330	Forward overhang component
FPD	325	Freeboard propeller depth
FS	328	Freeboard at stem
FSP	814	Forestay perpendicular
G	843	Gaff length
GD	311	Girth difference
GF	873	Foresail gaff
GSDA	327	Girth station difference aft
GSDF	327	Ditto forward
GY	860	Mizzen gaff
H	842	Hoist of gaff mainsail
HB	839	Headboard of mainsail
HBF	873	Ditto foresail
HBS	819	Ditto spinnaker
HBY	855	Ditto mizzen
HC	847	Gaff hoist corrected
HF	873	Hoist of gaff foresail
HFC	873	Ditto corrected
HY	859	Hoist of gaff mizzen
HYC	863	Ditto corrected
I	809	Height of foretriangle
IC	829	Ditto corrected
IS	880	Height of schooner mainmast
IY	858	Height of mizzen mast
J	807	Base of foretriangle
JC	826	Ditto corrected
L	334	Rated length
LBG	327	Length between girths
LBGC	331	Ditto corrected
LL	828	Luff limit of spinnaker
LLA	314	Limit of length aft
LOA	301	Length overall
LP	827	Longest perpendicular
LPG	813	Ditto of jibs
LPIS	815	Ditto of inner jib
MACG	517	Movable appendage CG
MAF	518	Movable appendage factor
MAW	516	Movable appendage weight
MD	326	Midship depth
MDI	335	Midship depth immersed
MDIA	336	Ditto adjusted
MDS	313	Mid depth station
MSA	803	Measured sail area
MSAT	844	Ditto of topsail
MSATF	873	Ditto of foretopsail
OF	876	Schooner foresail overlap
OMD	326	Outer mid depth
OMDI	335	Ditto immersed
P	837	Mainsail hoist
PC	846	Mainsail hoist corrected
PBW	607	Propeller blade width
PD	325	Propeller depth
PL	702	Pendulum length
PRD	606	Propeller diameter
PS	608	Propeller size
PSF	875, 878	Foresail hoist schooners
PSFC	873	Ditto corrected
PY	853	Mizzen hoist
PYC	862	Ditto corrected
RD	512	Rated draft
RM	708	Righting moment
RMC	709	Ditto corrected
RSA	804	Rated sail area
RSAB	882	RSA between masts schooners
RSAC	896	RSA combined abaft masts
RSAF	830	RSA foretriangle
RSAG	874	RSA schooner foresail
RSAK	869	RSA mizzen staysail
RSAM	850	RSA mainsail
RSAT	898	Total rated sail area
RSAY	864	RSA mizzen
RSBS 1–6	304	Rated sheer below sheer
S 1–3	Appx. I	Sides of mules and topsails
SATC	897	Sail area total correction
SBMAX	327	Length bow to BMAX
SDM	327	Length bow to draft station
SF	822	Spinnaker foot length
SL	821	Ditto luff/leech length
SMG	823	Ditto mid girth length
SMW	820	Ditto maximum width
SPD	327	Length bow to PD station
SPH	810	Spinnaker pole height
SPIN	831	Spinnaker rated area
SPL	808	Spinnaker pole length
√S	899	Square root RSAT or SPIN
ST 1–3	609	Propeller struts
TR	710	Tenderness ratio
VHA	322	Vertical height aft
VHAI	322	Vertical height aft inner
WCBA, B	505	Centerboard weights
WCBC	506	Centerboard weight total
Y	327	Distance AGS to LLA
YSAC	870	Combined RSA mizzen sails
YSD	867	Mizzen staysail depth
YSF	866	Mizzen staysail foot
YSMG	868	Mizzen staysail mid girth

Part III
HULL MEASUREMENTS

301. Length Overall (LOA). The length overall of a yacht will be measured to include the whole hull, but not spars or projections fixed to the hull such as bowsprits, bumpkins, pulpits etc. It will be measured from:

.1 A point forward being the forwardmost of the following points:
    A. The stem of the yacht, whether carried above deck level or not.
    B. The bulwarks of the yacht where these are extended above the stem.

.2 A point aft, being the extreme after end of the hull and bulwarks or taffrail of the yacht whether at, above, or below deck level. Rubbing strakes at the stern will be included. If rudder and/or push-pit extend abaft this point, neither one nor the other will be included.

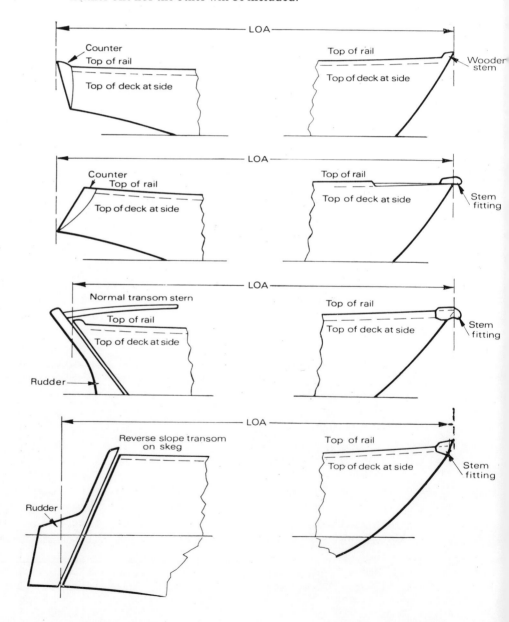

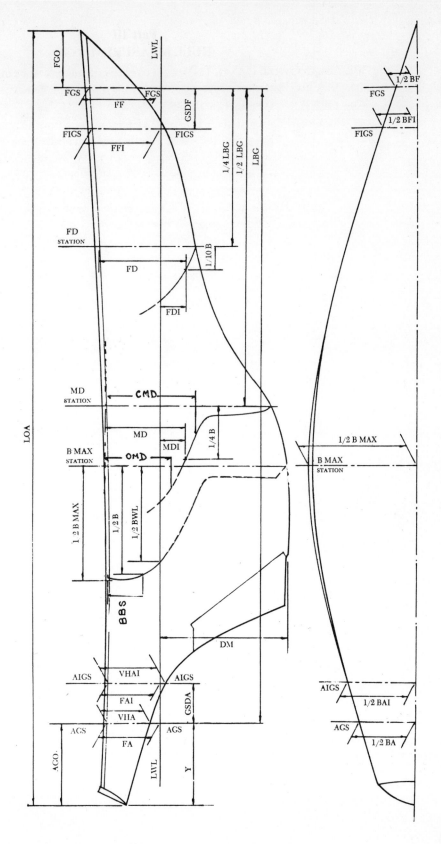

133

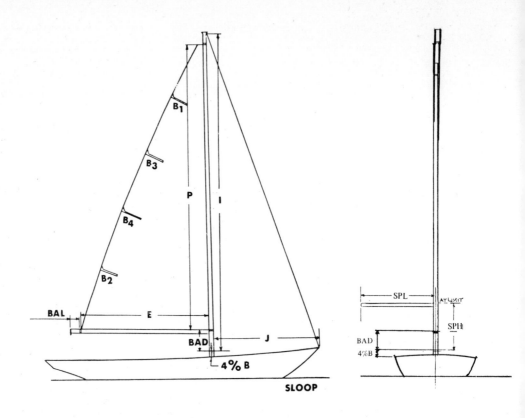

SLOOP

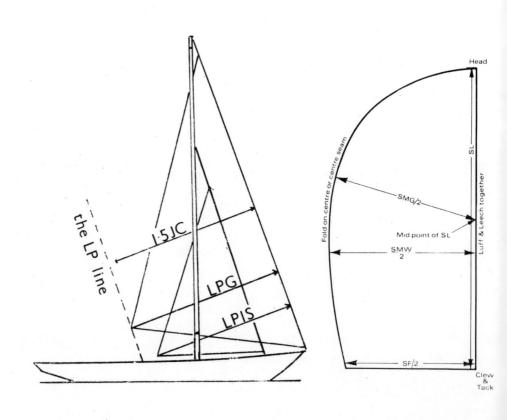

```
            INTERNATIONAL OFFSHORE RULE MARK II     *****************************
                                                    *NORYEMA
                                                    *****************************
I CERTIFY THAT I UNDERSTAND MY          DESIGNER_SPARKMAN & STEVENS
RESPONSIBILITIES AS COVERED IN                      RATING CERT. NO.RORC113
THE INTERNATIONAL OFFSHORE RULE:  RIG- 1 1 MAIN
                                 RORC-              -ANCHORS-(LOC) --RAFTS--(LOC)
---------------------------------   SAIL NO.3023    1-35    F    1-112    A
R.W. AMEY                            STD.NO.      0  2-20    F    2-60     A
ROWLEIGH HOUSE,BESSELSLEIGH  CLASS SWAN 48         3-0.0         BALLAST-(LOC)
ABINGDON, BERKS.                    YR.BUILT1972                 1-0.0
TEL NUM                      MEASUREMENTS IN FEET AND LBS        2-0.0
-SAILS
  --MAINSAIL-    FORETRIANGLE   --MIZZEN-    BETWEEN MASTS SCHOONER
  E    16.470  I    60.000  EY    0.0   EB    0.0  OF    0.0  --MULE- -TOPSAIl
  P    54.000  J    20.070  PY    0.0   PSF   0.0  HBF   0.0  S1    0.0
  BAD   4.480  LPG  30.000  BADY  0.0   BADS  0.0  BS1   0.0  S2    0.0
  G      0.0   LPIS  0.0    IY    0.0   BADX  0.0  BS2   0.0  S3 0.0
  H      0.0   JC   20.070  GY    0.0   IS    0.0  BS3   0.0  -BETWEEN MASTS-
  BAL   0.500  IC   60.000  HY    0.0   GF    0.0  BS4   0.0      S4    0.0
  BD    0.500  LP   30.105  EB    0.0   HF    0.0  BS5   0.0      S5    0.0
  HB    0.460             BALY    0.0   EF    0.0  BLP   0.0      S6    0.0
  BL1   2.620  -SPINNAKER--         BALF   0.0              -MIZZEN STAYSAIl
  BL2   2.620  SPL  19.980  HBY   0.0                            YSD   0.0
  BL3   2.930  SPH  14.900  BY1   0.0                            YSF   0.0
  BL4   2.930  SL   60.000  BY2   0.0   S-BMAX  27.500           YSMG  0.0
  BL5    0.0   SMW  36.100  BY3   0.0   S-PD    38.570***********************
  BLP  12.000              BY4   0.0   S-DH    28.500*---RATED SAIL AREAS
  EC   16.470              BY5   0.0              *RSAF    902.587
  PC   54.000  HBS   0.0   BLPY  0.0              *RSAM    380.654
  BPEN   0.0                                      *RSAY      0.0
--------HULL MEASUREMENTS---------ENGINE AND PROPELLERS*RSAK    0.0
  LOA  47.980  FGO   3.160  FD   6.200  EW   640.000 *RSAC    0.0
  LWL  36.420  GSDF  2.040  MD   5.860  EWD   .7.550 *RSAB
  LBG  41.620  AGO   3.200  FF   4.960  PROD  1.400  *RSAD
  BMAX 13.570  GSDA  1.400  FFI  4.810  PF    0.850  *RSAG
  B    13.500  Y     3.200  FFD  4.290  PS    1.300  *RSAT   1283.241
  BWL  12.130  GD    0.0    FMD  3.820  PD    3.140  *SQ S     35.822
  BFI   4.450  VHA   3.140  FAI  3.690  BLADE WDTH 0.325 * -TYPE PROP INSTALL--
  BF    2.870  VHAI  3.680  FA   3.710  SHAFT LGTH       *
  BA    7.520  BAI   8.320  DM   7.790  TIP CLEARANCE    *
  BHA   2.280  BHAI  2.820  FOC  1.709  AOC  -0.248      *
                                                    *L    40.159  DB    7.823
-----CENTREBOARDS-----    ---RIGHTING MOMENT----    *D     6.033  MR   37.774
                          -WGT-   -WD-   -PD-   -PL- *DC  -0.009  FC   -0.146
  CD    0.0               100.0   25.35   3.60  175.00*EMF 0.0037 EPF  0.9789
  WGT   0.0     0.0       200.00  25.35   7.00  175.00*DF  0.0174
  CBD   0.0     0.0       100.00  26.12   3.60  175.00*RMC 1DEG HEEL    2205.
                          200.00  26.12   7.20  175.00*TR  31.535 CGF  0.9900
                                                    ********************
       WITH AGE ALLOWANCE OF 0.0% TCF=      0.8650 * RATING    36.6FEET  *
                                                    ********************
                                         BSF  594.6 * RATING   11.16 METERS
                                                    ********************

D. SANDERSON                    DATE    RATING SECRETARY    DATE OF EXPIRY
MEASURER NO.                    RORC
DATE MEASURED   0/ 0/ 0         72 BELLE VUE RD
                                SOUTHBOURNE
                                BOURNEMOUTH

IJT2191
```

A typical rating certificate – that of Noryema VIII *is included.*

Index

Page references in *italic* denote illustrations